happy go money

MELISSA LEONG

HAPPY GO MONEY

SPEND SMART, SAVE RIGHT & ENJOY LIFE

Published by ECW Press
665 Gerrard Street East
Toronto, Ontario, Canada M4M 1Y2
416-694-3348 / info@ecwpress.com

Editor for the press: Jen Knoch
Cover art and design: Jessica Albert
Author photo: Greg Tjepkema

LIBRARY AND ARCHIVES CANADA
CATALOGUING IN PUBLICATION

Leong, Melissa Win Yun, author
    Happy go money : spend smart, save right and enjoy life / Melissa Leong.

Issued in print and electronic formats.
ISBN 978-1-77041-472-3 (softcover)
ISBN 978-1-77305-281-6 (PDF)
ISBN 978-1-77305-280-9 (EPUB)

    1. Money—Psychological aspects.
    2. Finance, Personal—Psychological aspects.
    3. Happiness. I. Title.

HG222.3.L46 2019   332.024
C2018-905331-3   C2018-905332-1

The publication of *Happy Go Money* has been generously supported by the Canada Council for the Arts which last year invested $153 million to bring the arts to Canadians throughout the country, and by the Government of Canada. *Nous remercions le Conseil des arts du Canada de son soutien. L'an dernier, le Conseil a investi 153 millions de dollars pour mettre de l'art dans la vie des Canadiennes et des Canadiens de tout le pays. Ce livre est financé en partie par le gouvernement du Canada.* We also acknowledge the Ontario Arts Council (OAC), an agency of the Government of Ontario, and the contribution of the Government of Ontario through the Ontario Book Publishing Tax Credit and the Ontario Media Development Corporation.

Ontario
Ontario Media Development Corporation

ONTARIO ARTS COUNCIL
CONSEIL DES ARTS DE L'ONTARIO
an Ontario government agency
un organisme du gouvernement de l'Ontario

Canada Council for the Arts

Conseil des Arts du Canada

Canadä

PRINTED AND BOUND IN CANADA   PRINTING: FRIESENS   5 4 3 2 1

MIX
Paper from responsible sources
FSC
www.fsc.org   FSC® C016245

To Jet

*If someone put a dollar figure on how happy you
make me, I'd be a Kardashian.*

To Mom and Dad

*You gave me everything and more.
I hope I make you happy.*

CONTENTS

INTRODUCTION

Dumplings. Spinach cake. The psych ward.

Sounds like the plot for a cooking show gone wrong, but each represents a period in my life that showed me the connection between happiness and money.

The first was when I was 29, and I was working as a crime reporter for a national newspaper. I hated covering crime so much that I fled the country. I took a three-month sabbatical and accepted a university scholarship to study in Taiwan with a small monthly allowance to cover food and rent. Once there, I lived out of a suitcase and shared a 200-square-foot underground apartment with a pack of cockroaches who kept me up at night, rustling plastic bags and flinging their crunchy bodies against the walls. My bank account, every month, was a ticker clicking from $1,000 to zero, and my new friends would join me in counting down like it was New Year's Eve.

That was one of the happiest times in my life.

Every day, I would wander, hike, study and eat. I gained the requisite "freshman 15." If I saw a lineup at a food stall or restaurant, I'd just join it. And as long as the food didn't resemble anything I'd slap with my flip-flop, I'd eat it. My meal of choice? Dumplings. Pan-fried dumplings; soup-filled, steamed dumplings. There, a plate of dumplings and a drink cost about $1.25. I filled my days (and my stomach) with joy and adventure and people — and I didn't worry about money or buying stuff.

The second period starts with a dumpling. Well, someone who I call my dumpling. My son was born in 2015 at the height of my career. I was back at my beloved newspaper, covering personal finance, and appearing on my favourite national talk show. I had just gotten a salary boost. I was two books into a self-published teen trilogy that had sold more than 70,000 copies. And then in my off-off hours, I made extra bucks teaching and performing dance. I was sprinting with no time for rest or liquids because, I mean, who has time to sleep or pee? Those boxes on my career and financial checklists weren't going to tick themselves.

When my maternity leave ended, I scheduled a meeting with my editor-in-chief. Would I be coming back full-time, part-time or not at all? Time away to raise kids can screw with your career and your earning potential, both of which were important to me. (Mothers who took more than three years off earned 30% less than childless women at age 40, one Statistics Canada report says.)

The day before my meeting, I was still figuring out what to do and baking healthy treats for my little guy. By baking, I mean randomly mixing flour, eggs and vegetables. I'd finally found someone who enjoyed my culinary art; he obviously knows that my oven bakes good buns. Catching everyone, including myself, off guard, I decided to quit my job.

I just wasn't ready to go back. I wanted to be at home to make my kid zucchini muffins, yam cookies and spinach cake. It cost me a $65,000 salary (and an $8,000 maternity leave top-up that I had to pay back immediately). But I bought over 2,500 more hours with my son (assuming each day I worked eight hours and commuted for two). Buying this time with my family has brought us so much joy. I can no longer say the same about the spinach cake.

Finally, the third episode in my life that taught me my most important money lesson began a few months after I got married. My husband had gotten a prescription for sleeping pills for a guys trip where they'd all be sleeping (and snoring) in the same suite. What ensued was what may be considered one of the worst times in my life — and his. My husband suffered terrible side effects after taking the pills. He quickly became buried under the crushing weight of depression and terrified by relentless anxiety and suicidal thoughts. Very suddenly, my beautiful, outgoing, make-me-laugh-until-I-cry husband disappeared into someone I did not recognize.

I made it my mission to keep a strong hand extended into a dark hole. And to be happy in the face of it. Not easy when I've always said that the glass was half-empty — probably because I've spilled milk and now I'm crying over it. Friends called me Negatron. I have a depressing factoid handy to counter every happy ending: divorce rates, crime numbers, cancer statistics. (Yes, I'm available to entertain at your next party.)

But I became a joy ninja. I learned to meditate. I pored over every book I could find on the study of happiness and positive psychology. I consumed hours of lectures from Buddhist monks and resilience gurus. They talked about mantras and gratitude exercises and anti-inflammatory, mood-boosting diets — all of which I tried — and no one talked about finances. But I knew that I could focus on happiness and my husband could focus on healing — which he had time to do because we had our money shit in order.

So, absolutely, money and happiness are connected. But not necessarily in the way we think. Everything tells us that what will make us happy can be bought. Bliss is a click away with this online purchase. The average city-dweller sees thousands of ads a day — a tsunami of commercials, billboards, brand names, pop-ups, celebrity endorsements and more. Meanwhile, social media shows us a curated checklist of lifetime accomplishments, travel destinations, meals and new outfits deserving of selfies. We drag around our student debt for years after graduating. We cower under surging house prices. We feel crappy about not saving enough, about spending too much, about not understanding our money or maybe not wanting to understand. And we just wish we had more. No matter how much we have. We just wish we had more.

The truth is more money doesn't always mean more happiness. You could be stuffing your joy bank with coins, and yet it remains empty. Don't worry. I got your back. I'm going to help you chart your own path to happiness with your money and life. Each chapter in this book ends with actionable tidbits — stuff you can do right away and then pat your back about. Also, I know talking money is tough, so I've provided questions to ask yourself or to discuss with others.

As great company as I am (I'm a fab wing girl/background karaoke singer/tucker-in-of-tags), I want you to find another means of support. This book is for you and a friend or friends because happiness is easier with a team. If you want to be happier and more successful with your goals, I encourage you to read this with your partner, bestie, office wife, a trusted group of peeps, whoever. Form a club, IRL or online — your very own "Oh Happy Money" community, which I'll refer to as your OHM tribe.

Your OHM tribe is your happiness and money-savvy support group. I suggest that you check in with each other (once a week over email, maybe once a month over a bottle of wine) and hold each other accountable to your goals. Talk about money. Yes, money makes people weird (because it's not about dollars and cents; it's about your identity, family, vanity, values, etc.), so I'm not saying that you must disclose your salary or your debts to everyone, but you can announce that you have a savings goal and every week or month discuss whether or not you've achieved it.

Read, highlight and dog-ear the pages of this book. Make notes in the margins because your own insights define your journey. Keep me updated on your progress and reach out to me with questions or for a digital high-five (@lisleong on Twitter and Instagram).

I'm not going to tell you to give up your daily latte. I'm not going to suggest that you forgo a new cellphone or that you don't upgrade to the bigger home or give up your dream wedding. But let's get clear about what really makes you happy and what kind of life you want — and how to get that through smart spending, simple saving and taking control of your money. This book isn't necessarily going to make you crazy rich. But it will make your life richer. And at the end of the day, that's what we all really want.

BUYING HAPPINESS

*How we try to spend our way to smiles,
and what actually works.*

1
BANKING ON HAPPINESS

"If I only had a little more money, I'd be happier."

When was the last time that you had this thought? Every day, we make choices based on the idea that joy can be bought and that more money makes everything better. We take the new job with the extra hour in traffic because it pays more. We put a coat on credit because it's *designer*. We buy the big house because it has a yard for our future kids and a kitchen island that's "an entertainer's dream."

To be fair, scientifically speaking, when we see something we want, a new pair of shoes or a gadget, we do feel joy; it triggers a patch of tissue in the brain, the nucleus accumbens, the so-called sex and money area. It gets activated when humans receive a reward, whether drugs, money or food. Then when we buy something, we get a delicious burst of dopamine in the brain.

That sounds sexy and yummy and all, but the euphoria doesn't last. Then we just need more stuff. All that crap we buy loses its lustre. When the novelty wears off and the shopping high from the endorphin and dopamine dump dissipates, we're left with a void and possibly regret.

"Why did I spend money on this?!?" we ask. Because I need it. Because I deserve it. Because I had a rough day. Because I have no willpower. Because it was on sale. Because it's a habit. Because it was a whim, a knee-jerk reaction. But when you get down to it? Because I want to be happy.

So, what do we actually need to be happy? Let's break down our thoughts on the subject and rebuild. This is me swinging on a wrecking ball (fully clothed) to help.

The magic number

We all need a certain amount of money to be happy. But how much?

For those of us who are on the verge of losing our homes, who fret about feeding our children, who cringe when the phone rings because debt collectors may be calling, without question, more money will make us happier. But for the rest of us, before connecting cash with joy, we need to talk about what we mean by "happy."

Scientists in neuroeconomics (the study of how we make economic decisions) break happiness into two types:

1. **Life satisfaction:** an evaluation of your well-being as a whole (the kind of happy where you're pleased with life in general).
2. **Day-to-day mood:** the highs and lows; the joy, stress, sadness, anger and affection that you

experience from one moment to the next — how you feel today, how you felt yesterday. (The kind of happy that most of us relate to — the right now happiness.)

With life satisfaction, the richer people got, the more satisfied they were with their lives. In worldwide studies, people in richer countries reported higher life satisfaction than those in poorer countries. (We should also consider that wealthier countries are more politically stable, more peaceful and less oppressive — which affects well-being.) But according to a 2018 Purdue University study, there was a limit: $95,000 U.S. (pre-tax, per single-family household). Above that, more money didn't mean that you were more satisfied. With day-to-day happiness, the threshold is $60,000 to $75,000 per household, according to various studies. The 2018 study showed that after these salaries are met, life satisfaction and day-to-day happiness actually slightly decrease with more money.

What the what?

Well, apparently, when all of our basic needs are met, we become driven by other desires such as chasing after more material stuff and comparing ourselves to others, which make us unhappy. Also, high incomes can come with high demands (more working hours, more stress and less time with family and for leisure).

This doesn't mean that we should all go out and try to make exactly $75,000 a year — our so-called feel-good financial sweet spot. The studies are averages, and we all need different things to be happy. But *all* of us find joy in some simple things — kisses, laughter, getting IDed over the age of 25.

Marketing professor Hal Hershfield once told me, "Even if I have an amazing car in my driveway, a huge house and a big fat income, that doesn't necessarily mean that I'll be happier on a day-by-day basis, because the types of things that influence happiness are who I interact with, how I spend my time and the things that I do."

Think of some of your happiest times in the past week. Were you spending it with people? Were you taking time to enjoy an activity, going for a run or catching up with a good friend? Would a wad of cash have made those moments that much better?

Probably not. If you answered "yes" to the latter question, how much more do you need to be happy? Read on.

Your magic number is probably wrong

Let's do an exercise together.

How happy are you on a scale of one to ten?

Now think about how much money you have in the bank, your salary. How much more money would you need to be a perfect 10?

Michael Norton, who teaches at Harvard Business School and co-authored *Happy Money: The Science of Smarter Spending*, surveyed average-income earners and high-net-worth Britons (with a net worth of more than $1 million), and he asked them those questions. "Everybody said two to three times as much money," Norton told me.

"Why is that a problem?" I asked, estimating the same for myself.

"That's a problem because people at $1 million said, 'If I had $3 million, I'd be a perfect 10. Except that people who had $3 million said, 'If I had $9 million, I'd be a perfect 10.'"

Basically, happiness is on a sliding scale. Think about

how much this sucks. No matter what you have, you'll always want more. Even if you have millions. When you find the gold at the end of the rainbow, the pot is just too damn small, and then you're off again, chasing more rainbows.

It's like a curse really. It also takes the fun out of my childhood dream of winning a million-dollar lottery. That was the very first fantasy I ever had: winning a jackpot and marrying one of the New Kids on the Block (anyone but Danny). I'd have fancy clothes and we'd eat at Red Lobster every weekend. (Still my idea of a hot date today.)

But despite what we may think, winning the lottery doesn't buy you a one-way ticket to Euphoria Town. Take this famous study from 1978 where researchers asked two very different groups about their happiness: recent Illinois State Lottery winners who scored $50,000 to $1 million and recent victims of catastrophic accidents who were now paraplegic or quadriplegic. They asked the lottery winners and the accident victims to rate how happy they were at that stage of their lives, how happy they were before the life-altering event and how happy they expected to be in a few years. They asked them to rate how pleasant they found simple activities (talking with a friend, watching TV, eating breakfast, buying clothes, getting a compliment, etc.).

Seriously? Who's happier, the person cruising in the wheelchair or in the Lamborghini?

Yes, the lottery winners were happier in the moment. The winners reported feeling more present happiness. But the people with disabilities rated their future happiness higher. They also enjoyed the simple things in life more: they had more appreciation for the mundane pleasures of things such as hearing a joke or reading a magazine.

Actually, research shows a link between high income and

a reduced ability to savour small pleasures. Experts blame it on hedonic adaptation — our tendency to just get used to whatever we have. Even a dramatic life improvement eventually becomes the new normal. You don't smell the roses because they're everywhere, any time of the day. And research has shown that our inner thermostats are set somewhere between happiness and sadness: they can rise and fall depending on circumstance, but they generally return to that baseline. So, if you were a miserable moaner before hitting the jackpot, you'll likely just be a rich miserable moaner.

In another real-life example, Markus Persson, who created Minecraft and sold it to Microsoft for $2.5 billion in 2014, reportedly bought a $70-million mansion, complete with a candy wall, vodka and tequila bars, designer fire extinguishers (because safety first, fashion second) and 15 bathrooms equipped with $5,000 remote-control operated toilets with air deodorizers and heated seats. But in 2015, he tweeted, "Hanging out in Ibiza with a bunch of friends and partying with famous people, able to do whatever I want, and I've never felt more isolated." In another tweet, he said, "The problem with getting everything is you run out of reasons to keep trying, and human interaction becomes impossible due to imbalance."

Now this could be super depressing to you. For me, it's reassuring. It tells me that no single event or any material thing or external factor ultimately defines my happiness. Human beings are adaptable. A million dollars or a misfortune, over time, can become the new normal. Sure, with money, you'll enjoy stylishly fighting fire with your Louis Vuitton extinguisher, but the riches may also make old pleasures seem less enjoyable.

So remember, there's a better use of your money than

playing the lottery. The odds of winning the Powerball jackpot prize is 1 in 292 million — and odds are that more money won't guarantee that your days will be happier anyway.

YOUR HAPPY MONEY TO-DO LIST

- If you find yourself thinking, "If I only had [insert anything], I'd be happy," challenge it. Ask your partner or co-worker or friend to poke you (lovingly) if they ever hear you say that phrase. It'll be like that awful baby shower game where you can't say "baby" — but for your life.
- If you're relying on something (or someone) to make you happy, you're wasting your time and energy. If affirmations are your jam, write this down and stick it somewhere: "I control my own happiness."
- Name three big things that make you happy regardless of money (good health or a loving partner). Now name three very specific things (sleeping in on the weekend, your jam on repeat). Repeat the exercise every time you feel crappy about your financial situation — or any situation.
- Stop playing the lottery. Now. Next time you want to play the lottery, buy someone a coffee or put the money into a donation box instead for a guaranteed happiness payoff.

MONEY TALKS

- If you think more money would make you happier, how much more?
- How would your life be better with more money?

- Think of a time when you made less money. Were you unhappier then? How much?
- Think of some of your happiest moments from the last week. Would more money have made those moments better?

2
F*CK THE JONESES

Happiness often stems from expectations. And happiness is relative. Three of my husband's closest friends got sporty cars. And he did too. We have a Mercedes OMG something or other hibernating in our garage over the winter. (By the time you read this, I hope he'll have sold it, which he said he would — maybe because he finished reading this book and admits that it doesn't make him as happy as he thought it would.)

If everyone in my group of friends is carrying expensive purses, I might be more apt to splurge on a designer purse. If every post in my Facebook feed is someone's kitchen renovation, I might look upon my tired fridge and wish for one with a wifi-enabled touchscreen.

I'm not immune. When an acquaintance bought a new

home, I pulled up in front of her house and, through the front window, I saw a shining chandelier; I stared at the cascade of silver jewels dangling from a massive shade, and a voice in my head whispered, "I must have that." When I looked into the cost of that light fixture, the voice in my head yelled, "Holy mother of crap. That's a lot of money!!!" But I wanted to feel that awe in my house; I wanted others to admire my crap. And if she could afford it, surely I could too.

I bought it. It cost a quarter of my month's pay, which I now realize would've been better spent on other priorities. I also walk by that chandelier every day, and I don't even notice it anymore.

I later found out that the acquaintance had furnished some of her new house on credit — one of those "don't pay for 12 months" deals. That's the thing. Maybe your friend has a new car but zero savings for his family's future. Maybe your neighbours have a brand-new kitchen but paid for it on credit. You just can't know someone's situation from an Instagram post.

But based on our limited information, we compare, we covet and we compete. No wonder we struggle sometimes to be happy.

Beyond comparison

Would you compare yourself to a lottery winner?

No. That's ridiculous, right? But a 2016 study done for the Federal Reserve Bank of Philadelphia found that the neighbours of lottery winners are more likely to declare bankruptcy within a few years of the big win. Whether you live in a high- or low-income area, if you live beside someone who's won some money, you are more apt to ramp up your own spending on visible assets like cars.

Even when it clearly doesn't serve us, we use our peers as a standard for our own happiness. Almost half of respondents in a survey of faculty, students and staff at Harvard preferred to live in a world where the average salary was $25,000 and they earned $50,000 than one where they earned $100,000 but the average was $200,000.

Also, we're happy to do well, but we don't like to see others doing better than us. Psychologist Sonja Lyubomirsky did a study where she evaluated an unhappy group of people on a task and then told them how they fared against peers. They either heard A or B:

> A. "You got a crappy evaluation, but a peer did even crappier."
>
> B. "You got an awesome evaluation, but a peer did better."

Who was happier? Those who heard A. Yeah. Those who were told they did crappy.

Pretend you're an Olympic runner for a second. That means that you'd be happier if you missed your best time and your competitor went face first into the dirt than if you had won silver.

Put away the yardstick. You will always lose in a game of comparisons. Even if you're Miss America, there will always be a Miss Universe. And Miss Universe isn't Miss Universe forever.

Know that your brain naturally makes comparisons. Psychologists have long studied the good and bad of our innate tendency to compare. It's how we cope, build resilience and establish our identities, but it can also lead us to feel envy, guilt, regret. It can make you terribly unhappy and distract you from what matters, which is you focusing on you. And be aware of what you're putting out into the world. You might *be* the Joneses, in which case, if people are looking at you, what do you want to inspire in them?

F*ck the Joneses (with love)

Whenever I feel any kind of negativity toward someone, I try to kill the feeling with kindness. This isn't about being the nicest person in the country; this is about self-preservation. It's been said that resentment is like drinking poison and waiting for the other person to die. That person who I'm jealous of or angry at could give two butts about me; she's probably never going to get diarrhea while giving a presentation at the office or develop a permanent crotch itch — no matter how many times I've mentally wished it upon her.

I'm basically stewing in my fury, flogging myself with every evil thought about her. Think of the grudges you've held (or are holding). Who really suffers? Researchers at the National University of Singapore asked people to recall incidents where they were wronged and then asked them to jump five times, as high as possible, on a yoga mat. Those who had forgiven their perpetrators jumped higher than those who still held their grudges. It's like me after an all-you-can-eat Brazilian steakhouse meal — literally weighed down by beef.

There's a saying that goes, "Living well is the best revenge." No. No, it isn't. Moving on is the best revenge. Being successful just to spite someone is stupid. I remember all of these people who would go on daytime talk shows to confront an old flame or someone who was mean to them in high school; the victim would have gone from "geek to chic" or would now be rich and sexy and want to rub it in the other person's face. I always thought, uhh, maybe that other person doesn't give a crap about you. Maybe if you were really "chic," you'd have nothing to prove to anyone but yourself.

So instead of adding fuel to my grievances, I imagine that my nemeses too have a story of ups and downs and that they only want to be happy. Then I drink an antidote — I'll write an encouraging note on their Facebook wall, I'll invite them for coffee, I'll offer them help. For me. Not for them.

Whenever you feel the itch of jealousy, the sting of inadequacy, give yourself a shake. Quickly name three things that you've got going for you in your life. Anytime you feel envy, think of it as a prompt to ask yourself, "Why do I envy this person?" It might inspire some changes in your life.

I often suffer from impostor syndrome. When I was younger, impostor syndrome made me spend money on things to make me appear more professional — a suit jacket with the perfect shoulder pads, the sleek but functional work/life handbag. Today, impostor syndrome makes me vulnerable to envying someone's intelligence or talents.

"That person is so knowledgeable!" I'll say to my husband. "I need to be more like this guy."

He gets so annoyed. "Maybe that guy needs to be more like Melissa Leong."

Everyone on social media is a big fat liar

The next time you're scrolling through social media, stop and assess. Do you feel happy? Some studies have found Facebook use to be associated with a decline in happiness. One University of Michigan study reveals that the more research participants used Facebook over a two-week period, the more dissatisfied they felt over time. Was it because their newsfeed was filled with stories about murder and mayhem ("This 10-part series about war crimes against children is a must-read")? Or was it because their feed was filled with humblebrags ("Darn! Forgot to pack sunscreen for the French Polynesia #BoraBoraForBrains" or "Clutz alert! Just spilled red wine on my new coat")? The research out there is still incomplete. But in the meantime, if you're thinking, "Man, everyone is living it up except me" — it's not everyone, it's not all the time and it might all be a show. The internet lies.

You can rent a private grounded jet to take Instagram photos in it for about $250. In Las Vegas, while the budget hotel Circus Circus and the posh Bellagio hold the same number of people, the Bellagio gets about three times the check-ins on Facebook, an economist noted. Also, if someone owns a BMW, Mercedes or other luxury ride, they're more likely to show it off online.

We curate our lives for social media. We filter the crap out of photos. We filter our whole lives. We crop out the unsavoury parts of our vacations. We live-tweet the music festival but not the moment when the credit card is declined at the grocery store a month later. This is not reality. This is a reality TV version of life.

So many times, I've recognized the falseness in my own feeds. During my maternity leave, I mostly put up photos of me appearing on TV once a month. Friends would say, "You're so busy with all of your work," but I spent every other day of the month in a robe being a milk dispenser. My husband would take a day off from his work (he runs his own company) to look after the kid and I would go downtown for hair and makeup and live television. One day, I was on TV talking about credit scores and, based on my appearance and the photos, you'd never know that that morning I had been at the hospital until 5 a.m. with a sick baby. (The only blip was me making up the word "imaginatary" on live television.)

Don't base your feelings, your assumptions on a sliver of someone's life. With the masses all putting on their own show, with some using status updates to up their social status, we'd all be better off if we spent more time in the real world (versus an imaginatary one).

Celebrity worship syndrome

A few years ago, I asked my teenage niece what she wanted to be when she was older. She responded immediately.

"A VP?" I said. "That's great. A VP of what kind of company?"

"No, a VIP," she said.

"What is that?"

"Someone who's rich, gets into parties and gets free clothing."

WTF.

In the U.S., 81% of 18-to-25-year-olds said their most important or second most important life goal was getting rich — 51% said "being famous," according to a poll released in 2007. Incidentally, that's the same year that *Keeping Up with the Kardashians* debuted. We still watch that show and the Real Housewives — of Orange County, of Auckland, of Vancouver or wherever. There are the "Ultra Rich Asian Girls" on YouTube and the Rich Kids of Instagram. And, of course, celebrities. Celebrity faces boost the sales of everything from cosmetics and clothing to movies and Broadway plays. It isn't just a North American phenomenon; after a

Yves Saint Laurent lipstick was featured in a popular Korean television show, it sold out internationally.

We worship, we obsess, we emulate.

Seeking role models isn't unusual; even monkeys emulate the dominant primate in their group. But we're not monkeys. We can recognize how such influence taints our fountain of joy.

But instead we obsess over these superhumans who seemingly have it all. Our goal is to also be rich and famous because then we'll have everything, we'll be able to rub it in our enemy's face, we'll never suffer again. But what's after happily-ever-after? And who are we if we don't achieve this dream?

I was in my early 20s when I watched Mariah Carey tour her 11,000-square-foot Tribeca penthouse for MTV's *Cribs*. She glided from her living room to her lingerie closet, the decor and upholstery the colour of champagne; the walls, a shiny coral, glazed like candy. I thought, "Man, that woman has it all: talent, fame, fortune, a chaise longue in her kitchen." (So many times, I too have wanted to lie down while eating my meals.) But around that time, the singer also famously sought psychiatric treatment following an emotional breakdown.

That's always stuck with me. It didn't matter how many couches she had in her kitchen or how many rooms she had for her panties. It didn't protect her from the trials and tribulations of being human. It didn't safeguard her health. It didn't solve all of her problems. We like to believe that there's a group of people who walk in the sun, who have it all, who have truly achieved — because then we have something to hope for; we hope that we too can have it all.

But envy gnashes away at our happiness. Instead of comparing ourselves to others, we need to be grateful for what we have, focus on the opportunities ahead of us and turn off our phones and get a life outside of the glow box.

YOUR HAPPY MONEY TO-DO LIST

- Spend more time with people who are uplifting. When you hang with those who are always trying to compete with you or encourage you to spend, use a mental disclaimer like, "F*ck you, Jones. But I still love you."
- When you feel jealous, ask yourself, "Why do I envy this person? Do I know their story?"
- If you must compare, identify a money role model. Think about what they've done to succeed. What behaviours or qualities led them to where they are today? How can you be more like them?
- Choose who you see in your social media feed wisely. Unfollow (you can mute their posts but stay friends) or unsubscribe from anyone who makes you feel crappy. And add, like and engage with people whose posts align with your goals and values.
- If you find yourself mindlessly scrolling through your social media feeds, stop and ask, "Is this feeding my brain happy food, or will I suffer a social media hangover?"
- Start sharing things on social media that reflect your reality — the good and the bad — and your values. Be a source of good online.
- Unplug for the weekend or make a rule of no social media at the dinner table or set an alarm to limit your scrolling time to 15 minutes. When

you get together with friends or your OHM tribe, announce a social media break after you all take pictures of each other or your food or this book and then post or tweet or like them. Then put the phones away for the rest of the time together and enjoy the company.

- Consider using a screen-time tracker to help you limit and manage your usage. Agree to a digital diet with friends — a contest where you stay under a certain limit for a week.

MONEY TALKS

- Name something in life that you're proud of. Is your pride based on your own goals or on standards set by others?
- Describe the last time that you felt jealous of someone's financial situation or possessions. How did you handle it?
- Have you ever bought anything or spent money on anything to show off on social media? Have you ever purchased something that you thought you "should" have, something that would transform you into a better person?
- Share one of your happiest memories that were not captured on social media, maybe something from your childhood.

3
MORE STUFF? STUFF IT

My husband really, really likes stuff. The title of his autobiography should be *I Online Shop, Therefore I Am*. At least once every other week, I'll come home to find a box crowding our doorway. "More orders from online?" I'll yell into the house. So hereafter, I will refer to him with the acronym MOFO.

Ever since he was a boy, Mofo has wanted a sports car. His friends send each other car videos on YouTube and go for joy rides where they end up idling and admiring each other's rides in a strip mall parking lot. There isn't a material good on this planet that fills me with the same excitement. Sure, I like shoes. But I can't imagine my best friend sending me an online shoe review and me rewatching the video three times and reacting with an orgasmic grunt. "Ohhhh, do you hear the sound of the heel on the sidewalk?"

But that's me.

I've tried to relate to Mofo's fixation on this depreciating asset (I get that it doesn't help when I call it that). I even turned to science. Evolutionary behavioural scientist Gad Saad once explained to me that the vehicle was a status symbol, an example of sexual signalling, an ostentatious display to attract a mate, like a peacock's feathers. That's why men make up the majority of car collectors and why 99% of Ferrari owners in North America are guys. "Only truly high-class guys can drive an Aston Martin," Saad says. "The young guys can pretend with their Mustangs, but they don't have the same big tail as me, so to speak."

"Dude, you already got the girl," I told Mofo, relaying the science. "A frugal girl. A girl who identifies cars only by colour. Who are you trying to impress?"

"It's for the love of driving," he said.

But I have a study to counter that argument too. Researchers at the University of Michigan and Peking University studied whether luxury cars did in fact bring more happiness. They asked drivers to recall their most recent commute or the last time that they drove their cars for at least 20 minutes. They then asked how they felt during those specific trips. Finally, they asked them about the kind of car they drove. The value of the car made no difference in how the drivers reported feeling.

Imagine, there you are in your [insert fancy vehicle here]. Now imagine that you're in traffic and you're late for your meeting and construction crews have just closed another lane and you're staring down a convoy of cars with red tail lights. Yep. You're unhappy in your fancy car.

Commuting is crappy whether you're in a Kia or a Cadillac, and driving becomes routine. The thrill of the new wears off whether it's a car, the latest iPhone or a new love interest.

That's right, Mofo. Even your ultimate purchase can lose its shine.

House of (things bought with) cards

While on the money beat for the *Financial Post*, I once referenced a family who bought an expensive home but filled it with patio furniture because they didn't have money left to furnish it. It was so important to them to have *that* home. Maybe it was in a prime school district. But maybe it said something about them. Our home is an extension of ourselves. We define ourselves by the art on our walls, the shine of our kitchens, the potted flowers on our porch.

During my sabbatical in Taiwan, my scholarship money covered school tuition and an apartment in a bustling night market, and my main worry was that my creepy crawly roommates would sublet my orifices while I slept. The unit was the size of my current kitchen, and it was barren. I think I had one pot, one plate and one cup. The only piece of decor was a bathmat. I didn't have any money to make it "a home." But as someone who's moved a lot, "home" lives in me and goes wherever I go.

Years later, the memories of cockroaches, Taiwanese minimalism and almost all of my 20s got erased when I gave birth. (It's like my kid pushed a reset button on the way out.) Mofo and I moved into a bigger house and we just filled it with more stuff. It became a shrine to the suburban dream and a warehouse for toys and mamaRoos/jumperoos/whateveroos. We got a Costco membership. An Amazon Prime membership. Every other week, it was like Santa came to our home dressed as the UPS guy with a pasta maker or a leaf blower or an Instant Pot. It's all stuff I never knew we even needed. The other day, my friend told me that she was admiring an $800 mirror that doubled as a wireless stereo system. Really? Because every time I look in the mirror, I wish I heard Beyoncé? ("Who run this motha?!?") I'd maybe pay $800 for a mirror that doubles as a wind machine.

If I look around the house and picture price tags on everything, I hear screechy Hitchcock violins. We're not happier. We just have more clutter, more crap to maintain and more of a need for creative storage. (It's an ottoman *and* a toy chest!)

When I drive through my suburban town, I see self-storage facilities at every other major intersection, and I shudder to think of all of the junk that we're accumulating. (Self-storage is a billion-dollar industry. A company is now building the world's largest storage facility in Toronto.) I too have boxes of stuff stored in other people's basements across the country, and I have no idea what's in them. And how much of what we buy just gets shuffled to the curb? According to Edward Humes's *Garbology: Our Dirty Love Affair with Trash*, each American throws away 7.1 pounds of garbage *every day* and 102 tons in a lifetime. At the end of our lives, we'd need one grave for our bodies, 1,100 for our trash.

None of us needs more stuff. We already have too much stuff.

Fancy Schmancy

Many of us buy like we eat and breathe. Compulsively, impulsively. And it's making us miserable. Research out of Baylor University has found that the more materialistic we are, the less satisfied we are with life. Higher materialism is associated with lower-quality relationships and lower-quality marriages. It's associated with less connection with others, with insecurity and with narcissism. One study published in the *Journal of Experimental Social Psychology* suggests that low self-esteem plays a part in determining whether someone will buy a luxury item that she cannot afford.

And what is luxury anyway? The mere fact that something is expensive makes it an indulgence, and our brains tell us that we should enjoy it more because of the hefty price tag — a brand-name white cotton shirt versus a generic one, for example. Both are 100% cotton.

It comes down to perspective.

When I was young, I thought lobster dinners were reserved for birthdays and death row meals. Hell, we served steak and lobster at our wedding — a meal which Mofo proudly called "lobeefster" — because it was the fanciest thing we could think of. But here's some food for thought: when European colonists discovered lobster, they regularly fed the bottom feeders to enslaved people, prisoners and the poor. People revolted, citing cruel and unusual punishment, leading Massachusetts to pass a law forbidding it from being served more than twice a week.

Perspective.

I'm not saying that we must lead a life of austerity, sell all of our possessions and start a commune in the woods. I'm not saying that all stuff is a waste of money — if your home is like a sauna in the summer, and you sweat like sizzling bacon while trying to sleep, buy an air conditioner. But we need to resist the harmful temptation to consume and collect. We have to stop consuming beyond our means, because the greatest happiness killer is debt. We have to ask, "Do I really like the taste of lobster? Do I enjoy eating the green goo inside its head that is considered a delicacy? Or do I like lobster because it's 'fancy'?"

Forget fancy. You'll be happier.

YOUR HAPPY MONEY TO-DO LIST

- You are not defined by your stuff. Consider a detox — a short period of only buying necessities. Determine your list of needs and avoid the rest. You decide how long: a week, a month, . . . See how you feel. Report back to me. For inspiration, check out Cait Flanders's book *The Year of Less* and Sarah Lazarovic's illustrated book *A Bunch of Pretty Things I Did Not Buy.*

- Inventory your stuff. If you know what you have, it might eliminate the need to buy more or the purchase of duplicates. Declutter and donate or sell unwanted items. (For example, I do a sweep of my wardrobe every year; if something hasn't been worn in three years, it will likely get the boot. Or put some stuff into a box and if you don't open it in a certain period of time, donate the whole box.)

- If you ever look at your stuff, like your wardrobe, and think you need a new one, consider that you might just be bored. After you buy something new, you might soon get bored again. Organize a clothing swap with your friends or OHM tribe. Want new decor around the house? Try rearranging the things you have so the space feels different, or swap decor too. Ask a friend to trade wall decor (maybe not your family photos) for six months or holiday decorations for a season.

- If you think you need something new, consider whether you can rent or borrow it. Libraries for things like tools, camping gear or kitchen equipment are popping up all over. As one borrowing enthusiast points out, "You don't need a drill; you need a hole in the wall." If something's broken, rather than tossing it, consider seeking out a repair café — meet-ups where people will help you repair everything from clothes to household electrical items for free. Or start one up in your community.
- When buying something new, ask yourself why you want the fancier option. If it's twice the price, will it last twice as long? Will the experience be twice as good?

MONEY TALKS

- What was the last item that you spent your money on? How happy did it make you?
- Name something you've bought within the last year that was a good investment and something that was a bad investment. Why was one good and the other a mistake?

4
BUYING HAPPINESS (FOR REAL)

You work hard for your money. It should make you happy. You deserve that.

But before you open your wallet, know that some things you buy stand to make you happier than others. Sure, we're all different. We enjoy different things and we tell ourselves different stories about what we should value. Mofo likes depreciating assets. And I like charcuterie boards and veiny cheeses made by Trappist monks.

But will buying a Happy Meal do the job? Ask someone else, and they might say that spending on meals is a waste, literally. How then, you might say, are you going to tell me what to buy when we're so unique? To help you achieve maximum joy with your dollars, I'm going to suggest three types of things to spend on:

1. Experiences
2. Time Savers
3. Anticipation

These things, according to research, will make you happier in the long run and give you a greater return on your investment.

Go and do versus get and own

If your home was on fire, what would you run back inside to save? If my family was safe on the lawn (my toddler would be trying to drive the firetruck), I would grab this yellow summer dress that I got on sale from a local designer and these cute elephant-shaped teapots from Kitchen Stuff Plus.

Ha.

No, seriously. I would drag out a box of journals. I've kept diaries since I was a kid. I have the worst memory. (Mofo says we're living out *The Notebook* where he has to remind me of what I like to order off a menu. My best friend had to dig up photographic proof to convince me that I had met J-Lo when we were teens.) My journals are a record of my experiences. At the end of the day, all that matters are our memories, our experiences and our relationships.

So, if you want to be happier, buy tickets to that summer music festival instead of a watch. Save for a sojourn in Stockholm versus a visit to IKEA. Spend your bonus on a spa weekend with mom in lieu of a Black Friday online shopping splurge. Sign up for a yoga class membership and not a membership to monthly yoga pants.

It's hard to put a price on life experiences — which is why we underestimate their power. Researchers at San Francisco State University found that shoppers, despite knowing that buying life experiences will make them happier than buying material items, still spent on things. "We naturally associate economic value with stuff. I bought this car, it's worth $8,000," associate professor of psychology Ryan Howell told the university's newsletter. "We have a hard time estimating the economic value we would place on our memories." (Dr. Howell founded a website called BeyondThePurchase. org, which studies the psychology behind spending.) Dr. Howell said that when happy people get a lump of free money, they spend 23% on consumer goods. They take 25% and save it or invest it. They give 12% to others or charities. And they spend 40% on life experiences.

Experiences make us happier because they make us feel more connected to others and the world. You'll also get more bang for your buck because experiences increase in value over time. The thrill of a new gadget will fade, but the memories and goodwill from a night out with friends will last. And you'll get repeated joy every time you retell the story. A 2014 study published in the neuroscience journal *Neuron* showed that people were willing to sacrifice money to remember and savour happy memories.

"Material things very often are enjoyed alone. Social relationships are the single most critical thing in our lives for happiness. Anything we can do with our money to enhance those relationships is a good thing," says Elizabeth Dunn, a professor of psychology at the University of British Columbia and co-author of the great book *Happy Money: The Science of Smarter Spending*.

I try to remember this on every birthday, Christmas and holiday. Before Valentine's Day, I remind my husband that I don't want overpriced flowers or a chocolate box shaped like cupid. (I already deal with a baby filled with brown treats.)

Let's spend that money on a date. Instead of gifts, my friends and I have brunch. Or we take an introductory archery course or do a painting night. Every year on my birthday, 10 of us go away for a spa weekend in a small town (what happens in Collingwood stays in Collingwood). We spend our money on laughter and happy endorphins from physical activity. I send invites to them with the hashtag #lovenotstuff. (Oh, the joys of being friends with a money nerd.)

Surveys suggest that millennials already prefer spending on experiences over things, and retailers are jumping on the trend to try to attract customers by hosting live performances or building cafés in their stores. (Just remember that you can enjoy the show without buying a new sweater.)

Money might also be better spent in helping you learn a new skill like creative writing or photography or surfing. By expanding your horizons, you're expanding the ways in which you can experience joy. It's a (not so) secret of mega-successful people: they continue to invest in themselves. They take self-improvement seminars. They take courses on public speaking or web development. They learn new languages or face their fears with an improv class or a rock-climbing lesson. It makes you more marketable in the job field, and it helps you earn more money for your goals and for joyful experiences.

Plus, experiences can improve your sense of self in a more lasting way — going on an adventure, climbing that mountain, learning that skill — how do you put a price on a feeling of accomplishment? Dr. Howell also found that with experiences, people were less likely to compare themselves to their peers. You can compare your car to Susie's car and feel happy or crappy about it, but you're probably not going to think, "Wow, I'm doing a better job than she is at relaxing in this hot tub."

Finally, look for new experiences. Couples who did new things together reported better relationships. Your brain is a novelty detector, neurologist Rick Hanson writes, looking for new, unexpected information and storing it rapidly. You'll be more likely to remember (and enjoy) unique experiences. You get top points for participation.

Buy a hot tub time machine or spend on time savers

What is more valuable to you: money or time?

Research from 2016, which had thousands of individual subjects, shows that people who value time over money are happier people. As a part of their experiments, scientists at the University of Pennsylvania and the University of California, Los Angeles, asked some people to focus on the value of time and others to focus on the value of money, with the former feeling happier as the result.

Think of it this way: if you lose a dollar, you can earn it again. If you lose a minute, it's gone forever.

So spend money on the things that will give you the gift of time. Try hiring someone to clean your house once a month or paying someone to do your taxes. Pay a babysitter so you can go out in public with other adults. Spend more to get the direct flight versus the route with two connections.

Mofo bought a robot vacuum on Amazon. Initially, I was livid that Mofo had spent hundreds of dollars on what looked like an oversized hockey puck. Resentful, I called it "the Little Idiot."

"The Little Idiot has locked itself in the laundry room again."

"The Little Idiot is in one spot chasing its own tail."

But the Little Idiot zooms around the house every day. Instead of vacuuming, which we hate to do, the robot does it. My kid turns it on himself after he's thrown his bread crumbs around like confetti. We spend that extra 20 minutes every other day with our son or doing something more valuable — like working on our businesses, like writing this book.

Dr. Dunn spent money on a night doula to help sleep train her baby. She told me that it was beyond worthwhile. Buying anything that improves the way you spend your time is money well spent, she says.

The researchers at the University of Pennsylvania and the University of California, Los Angeles, say that people who choose money over time are more likely to be fixated on not having enough. Meanwhile, time appreciators focus on spending any extra moments with other people.

Now if you're doing something to save money, but it takes a lot of time, it might not be worth it when it comes to happiness. For example, driving around looking to save a few cents on gas or waiting in line for 20 minutes at a festival to get a free popsicle won't add up when you put a value on your time.

Mofo has criticized me over the years for being penny-wise and pound-foolish, especially when it comes to my time. I've left a gas station and driven five minutes to another that had my bank's ATM to avoid a $3 ATM fee. I've filled out online surveys to get a coupon I might never redeem. Since going on a quest to be happier, I've changed my ways. I start with the questions, "Is this worth 30 minutes of my time? Would my time be better spent doing something else?"

Think about the work that you do. Is it a good use of your time? When you take a job that makes you more money, think about the time commitment involved and/ or the commute. Taking a job with an hour-long commute each way has a negative effect on happiness, similar to not having a job at all, Dr. Dunn says. And in their research paper "Stress That Doesn't Pay: The Commuting Paradox," Swiss economists Alois Stutzer and Bruno Frey found that people who commute an extra 23 minutes a day one way would have to get a 19% pay raise to be as happy as those without that extra travel time.

Yes, maybe a job out of town every other Saturday for a year would make you $5,000 extra dollars, but here's another way to think about it: would you pay $5,000 to spend an extra 26 days with your family?

The anticipation is thrilling you

Remember how excited you were as a kid to count down to summer vacation? As adults, we have the power to recreate this excitement. We can pay for anticipation. In a 2010 Dutch study, vacationers were happier before their trip than those not travelling, but in the weeks following, there was no difference in happiness levels between those who had gone on vacation and those who had not.

Quick, picture your celebrity crush. How much would you pay to kiss this person right now? Okay, how much would you pay to kiss them in three hours (you know, so you could go home and brush your teeth) or 24 hours or three days? A U.K. study from 1987 showed that people were willing to pay the most to kiss a movie star of their choice in three days. You want the time to bask in the expectation.

If you can save your money for something, you'll appreciate it more when you get it. If you can spend your money today on things for the future, it'll provide a bigger boost to your happiness. This is the opposite of what a lot of us are doing now, which is buying something immediately on our credit card and then paying for it afterward. We want instant gratification. We buy something online, and we want it delivered to our door the next day.

You might say, "Listen, Leong. I know you're trying to dress up delaying gratification. But delaying gratification doesn't make me happy in the moment."

But it does. Scarcity boosts appreciation. Making something a treat supersizes your happiness. Imagine having your favourite meal every day versus savouring it once a month. Only having it once in a while magnifies satiation because you're fostering hunger.

Willpower is a muscle that is built, and you're flexing your strength and building confidence every time you delay gratification. Also, when things or experiences are anticipated and special, it inspires you to take better care of them and spend more time with them.

Delaying gratification is tough. Otherwise, we'd all be our ideal weight, have stockpiles of savings and I wouldn't read the ending of movies on Wikipedia before I've finished watching them.

Distraction helps. Instead of resisting, pay attention to something else, like another pleasure. I don't mean skip the cake and have a chocolate bar. Just use your imagination and imagine the pleasure of indulging in it or something else. Or walk away and call a friend for some laughs.

And not every treat has to be a dream vacation. To be honest, the best part about the cake is the photo that you take of it for Instagram, then the first bite. After that, your pleasure diminishes as you get used to the taste and become satiated. You don't need to stuff the entire cake in your mouth to enjoy it more. Duke behavioural economist Dan Ariely performed an experiment in his classroom where he charged his students 25 cents per bite of pizza. The students stuffed the pizza in their mouths to save money, even though it reduced their enjoyment of the food. Hey, sometimes less is more.

YOUR HAPPY MONEY TO-DO LIST

- Invest in experiences. The memories are lasting and so are the social bonds formed or the skills learned. Make a list of things you'd like to learn or try. Cross-reference your list with a friend or with your OHM tribe to find a buddy.
- Minutes are worth more than money. Ask yourself, "Is this worth my time? Would my time be better spent doing something else?"
- Save for something or buy it now — but enjoy it later. Count down to a vacation or a dinner out with friends; send an email to your OHM tribe, for example, a week before your wine and cheese meeting and tell everyone how much you're looking forward to it. Plan two shorter trips this year rather than one long one, so you have two things to look forward to. Anticipation makes for happier days.

MONEY TALKS

- If you had an extra $100, $500 or $1,000, how would you spend it? If you had an extra hour, week or month of free time, how would you spend it?
- How would you spend a bonus differently than your regular salary?

- If you had unlimited money but only 24 hours to live, how would you spend your last day? What would be the most important components of that day, the three musts?
- Recall the last time that you savoured something. If you could, would you choose to have it every day?

CHECK YOURSELF
BEFORE YOU WRECK YOUR WEALTH

It's not you, it's me.
No, it's actually you. Figure out how your habits
affect your money moves.

5
WATCH YOUR FRIGGIN' LANGUAGE

In the thousands of interviews that I've done over the years, covering everything from crime to politics to film to finance, the hardest things to speak to people about are death and money. (Just wait for when we have to talk about death *and* money, coming atcha in a few chapters.)

People are loathe to talk to you about their money habits. They're ashamed to admit that they have no idea about finances. They refuse to tell you how much they make. Or they talk to you and then they regret it. I've had people under the threat of violence rant to me about political regimes without a second thought. Yet when someone tells me how much they spent on booze in a month, they might call me back 24 hours later, retracting their revelations. How you handle money reflects who you are — or who you tell yourself you are.

Also, how you talk about money, especially with yourself, determines how happy you can be when tackling your finances. So what are you saying about money? When you talk about money, is the Negatron speaking for you?

The people in my life either brag or bitch about finances — or say nothing at all. I have a friend who will point out the things that Mofo and I spend our money on and add, "Must be nice to have money." He'll also decline going out for dinners with the gang because his family "has cash issues." Dude, you have a new car. You support your family so that your wife can stay home. So why the poor-man's narration? What purpose does it serve to use that kind of language? If anything, I was always proud of him and his family's financial accomplishments.

But maybe every "Look at you, moneybags" makes him feel better about his choices. Or maybe it's his default response, a habit, something he learned from his parents. Or maybe he needs to think of himself as without to stick to his budget. (My father-in-law says, "The people with money cry, 'No money' — because that's how they keep their money.") But negative talk could be holding you back. And others. Your friends, your family, your children can absorb your cynical view of money.

I know it's tough to change your views. Psychologists talk about the stickiness of negative mental habits. In his studies at Ohio State University, John Cacioppo showed people photos that would arouse positive feelings (a Ferrari or a bowl of ice cream), negative feelings (a mutilated face) and neutral feelings (a plate, a hair dryer); meanwhile, he recorded electrical activity in the brain. The negative photos resulted in the biggest surge of activity. Two-thirds of your amygdala (your centre for emotions and motivation) is used to detect negativity, which it then stores in your long-term memory bank, says neurologist Rick Hanson. When the Negatron moves in, he scrapes himself a path in your brain on which he routinely commutes.

But psychologists also tout our neuroplasticity — our brain's wonderful ability to reorganize and form new neural connections. We need to build new pathways where Negatron cannot go. We need to retrain the brain to be more positive.

What do you say to yourself when you're presented with a money choice? Absolutely, you can say, "I can't afford this." That might be the truth. But this book is about happiness. If you're not empowered by the negative, let's get into some strategies for putting a positive spin on your money monologues.

Enrich your language

Focus on what you will get from your choice instead of what you won't. Rather than "I'm too broke-ass to buy this," try "I'm kicking my debt's ass."

Negatron might say, "I can't go out for dinner, guys, I have no money." Really, no money? Maybe you have money but you choose not to use it here. Give the mic to Optimist Prime instead: "I'd love to, but I'm saving for our March Break family vacation, and we're so damn close to our goal. Hit me up the next time you guys are getting together."

Or if your inner Negatron moans, "I *should* be saving more," let Optimist Prime remind you that it's your choice: "I *could* be saving more."

For more motivation, position your choices as either/or scenarios. Studies show that these scenarios are more effective in managing your money. In a 2009 study published in the *Journal of Consumer Research*, people were 20% less willing to buy a $15 DVD if the option to not buy it was described as "keeping money for other purchases." The choice to buy a 16GB iPod Touch (instead of a 32GB device) doubled when accompanied by the phrase "leaving you $100 in cash." When you're about to order takeout even though you have food at home to cook, think, "Would I rather spend this $50 on greasy chow mein or put this $50 toward saving for my vacation in three months?"

Do you have specific savings accounts or jars? Rename them to something meaningful, something motivating. Name your emergency fund "Don't worry be happy." Name your vacation fund "For awesome tan lines." Name your retirement fund "Live like George Clooney."

Remember personal finance is all about choices. You're not just saying "no." You're saying "yes" to something else.

Take it a step further and, in addition to the either/or scenarios, use the "some now, some later" thought process. For now, you're choosing to live more simply so that you'll have more for later. I often say, "You can have it all — just not all at the same time." Who wants to consume the entire buffet at once anyway?

Stop serving yourself the haterade
You: "I'm a financial dumbass."

Me: "How dare you talk about my new friend like that!"

Remember no one has the power to define you but you. Be very conscious of how you judge yourself when it comes to your finances.

If you think, "I'm terrible with money," know that that thought could strip you of confidence and motivation. I've interviewed and spoken to many people who've said those words to me — the majority of them young women. A student once introduced herself to me as a money dummy; she then went on to explain that she was working part-time and over the summer to cover school expenses, and that she's trying to avoid debt. She may have more to learn, but she doesn't sound like a dummy to me. She just sounds like someone selling herself short.

Don't condemn yourself as a lost cause. A lost cause would not be reading a book that will later outline debt reduction strategies and the benefits of a term insurance policy (uhh, say what is coming?). And don't label yourself a victim.

In the worst days when Mofo was unwell, on my bathroom mirror was a Post-it note that read in big block letters, "NO VICTIMHOOD." That shoved me to the next moment, the next day. Research shows that people who play the victim tend to view events as happening to them and therefore feel overwhelmed, ineffective and powerless. You are in control of your money situation. You can get control of your finances. Right now, you are in control. Nod and say yes.

YOUR HAPPY MONEY TO-DO LIST

- Aim for positive self-talk when it comes to your finances. Or, at the least, for every negative thing you say about your money, quickly say three positive things.
- Before you buy something, ask yourself, "Would I rather spend my money on something else?"
- Remember you're in control. You are always choosing how to use your resources, including time and money. Don't say, "Oh, I don't have

time for that." Think, "I choose to use my time in other ways" or "I am prioritizing something else." If a phrase doesn't sit right with you (for example, "I am prioritizing work over spending time with my spouse" or "I am prioritizing this concert over putting money aside in case my dog gets sick again"), re-evaluate your choice.

MONEY TALKS

- How would you describe your money situation and your financial challenges? Could you describe them in a more positive way?
- How did your parents talk about money? What did you learn from that?

6
WORRIES B-GONE

Whether you're rich or poor, wherever in the world you live, one of our biggest worries is money.

Hey, maybe you have a reason to worry. Maybe you're a temp worker living paycheque to paycheque. Or maybe you're Kanye West worried about being $53 million in personal debt ("Please pray we overcome," read his moving tweet). Everyone has challenges and issues and hang-ups.

But no one ever solved the world's problems with worry alone. And too much stress damages us. A 2016 study in the *Research on Aging* journal asked panelists to guess the ages of people photographed first in 1994 to 1995 and again in 2004 to 2005. Those who were under heavy financial stress looked like they had aged more. How's that for an infomercial? "Forget those anti-wrinkle creams that just don't seem to work. Try our new product, Money Worries B-Gone, formulated with budgets and insurance to rejuvenate and protect."

But before we tackle the practicalities of our money situation, we have to deal with our money fears and anxieties. I promise that having a less worried (and more youthful-looking) game face on will empower you as you move forward.

Fear Factor: Finance Edition

Listen, I know about worry and fears. When I was a kid, I thought my kindred Muppet spirit was Telly, *Sesame Street*'s resident anxiety monster. My fears followed me into slumber, and I had night terrors every night for a decade. When I blew out birthday candles, I didn't wish for ponies or toys; I wished for my parents to avoid debilitating illness and extended hospital stays.

In my 20s, I obsessed about failure. The marauding thoughts would paralyze me, and they usually began with what if. "What if my competitor scoops me on a story and I get fired? What if I can't find a journalism job and I end up in the quality control department of a deodorant company and spend my days sniffing armpits? What if my sense of smell is so inferior that I end up broke?"

My counsellor at the time helped me through three main exercises to manage my stress.

Exercise #1: Confront the worst-case scenario.

What if I end up broke?

Realistic answer: If I could not pay my debts, I could file for bankruptcy and slowly rebuild like one of my family members did more than 20 years ago. I could ask my parents if I could move back in with them and just work my ass off to get on my feet again. It would suck, but I'd survive.

Exercise #2: Create an inventory of resources and an emergency preparedness guide.

What do you have in your arsenal when it comes to your money Armageddon? When it comes to resources, you have internal resources (personal strengths, knowledge, experience, etc.) and you have external resources (family support, government benefits and financial counsellors, for example).

Internal resources: I'm a workhorse, and I would do whatever it took to jump-start a new career. I am resilient and I've been through tough times and I have survived without crumbling.

External resources: I have a lot of friends in various industries who could help me find another job. Although my mom and dad pretend like they wouldn't want me back at home (they drag a mattress up from the basement to put in the dining room when I come to visit), they'd love it. My little sister is still living with them, so they'd just have two big babies. (My dad still makes my sister's lunch and drives her to work. When she texts me to complain that Dad made her a sandwich with just white bread and a breakfast sausage, I reply, "Why the hell is Dad still making your lunch when you're a grown woman?" Though, in all honesty, I would love a sausage sandwich right about now.)

Emergency preparedness plan: I have some savings, but I will beef up that account so it can support me for a few months if I ever lose my job. That way, I can turn my nose up at the deodorant company's job offer.

Exercise #3: Monitor and record your crappy thoughts and then take a step back to assess.

Mental health workers have suggested cognitive-behavioural therapy (CBT) to both me and Mofo on many occasions, and we've found it helpful. The practice, which is used to treat a range of problems that includes anxiety and depression, helps you identify, question and even change the thoughts and beliefs that stress you out. You're not just trying to think positively; you're trying to investigate other possibilities that could lead to new solutions to change your behaviour.

Here's an example of a thought log, an exercise used in CBT. Disclaimer: I am not a therapist (although I play one when my friends call), so the sample below should not be taken as the complete approach. Also, evidence has shown that CBT is more effective when you have the support of a real therapist. But if this looks like it might be helpful, definitely look more into it.

Situation: The credit card bill arrived.
Rate your feelings by intensity out of 100: Fear (85). Shame (60).
The automatic thoughts that are running through your mind: "I'm never going to pay this off; I'm a craptacular failure."
Evidence that supports that thought: I owe *so much* money. I'm only making the minimum payments.
Evidence against that thought: I've been able to cut back and use cash instead of adding to the debt. I am committed to using the birthday money from my parents next week to pay down some of the balance.
More balanced thought: "Even though it might take a long time, I am motivated to pay off my debt."

Rate how you feel now: Fear (45). Shame (30).

Making Lemonade

One of my friends is a fabulous success in my eyes. She's had an illustrious career as a magazine editor and a fashion stylist. She mentors young entrepreneurs and has launched several companies. She's well travelled, well heeled (when it comes to her shoe collection) and remains debt-free. Yet she considers herself a financial failure.

"I don't own a house. I don't have a stable job. I don't have massive retirement savings. I'm so behind," she told me.

My friend (and possibly you) is using benchmarks that are outdated. Let's go through a few of them.

"I don't own a house."

One of the milestones in becoming a successful adult used to be buying your own house, though it wasn't always the case. Pew Research Center data shows that in 1940, about 36% of women and 48% of men aged 18–34 lived with Mom and Dad in America; but by 1960, only 24% of young adults were living at home. And though home ownership reached between 60% and 70% in the following decades, the trend is showing a decline, especially among young people. As of 2016, Americans aged 25–34 were 10% less likely to buy a home than those a decade earlier.

I don't envy anyone trying to buy a house in a big city today. Without the help of parents, first-time homebuyers are facing a monumental feat. In Toronto in 2017, the average house price was more than $800,000; a 20% down payment for a home would be $160,000. Who has $160,000 when you're just starting out in your career, possibly with tens of thousands of dollars in student debt? With the house prices being what they are, and with so many competing priorities, renting comes with benefits, such as more freedom and mobility. The cost of renting is much less than the cost of owning a home. With a house, there's maintenance, property taxes, utilities and the allure of renos. "But it's an investment," you say. "I'd be paying myself."

As a renter, you could pay yourself too — and come out on top of the homeowner, says Alex Avery, chartered financial analyst and author of *The Wealthy Renter*. As an annual investment return, Canadian housing has not done as well as the Canadian stock market during the last 25 years. The U.S. stock market also has had better overall returns historically. So if you're a disciplined renter, you could outperform the homeowner if you invest the savings from renting in the stock market, Avery says. Also, if you invest in stocks (over real estate), you'll have easier access to your money, more flexibility and face lower brokerage fees. Not too shabby for a renter.

"I don't have a stable job."

When it comes to full-time "stable" work, that too is in lower supply than for the previous generation. Canadians aged 25 to 54 were less likely to hold full-time jobs in 2015 than in the past two decades. According to the Freelancing in America survey, more than 50% of the U.S. workforce will be freelancers by 2027.

My dad worked for the city health department for 34 years. He was pleased when I told him that I just needed to work at my newspaper for another 35 years to get my pension.

"It was a joke, Dad." Newspapers in 35 years. Ha ha.

The benefit to having the same job your entire life is that it is easier to make plans and retirement savings are often automated. If you have a pension, count yourself fortunate. If your company matches your retirement contributions, consider yourself to be riding a unicorn. (You'd better be flying that magical animal into the clouds and maxing out your contributions. Free money. Go now. If you have no idea if your company has this option, go email your human resources rep or your boss right now. I'll wait here.) But if you're on contract, if you've sewn together a bunch of part-time jobs to produce a living wage, if you're relying on your side hustle delivering for Uber Eats, then it's harder to be "winning."

But this is okay too. You can trade stability for flexibility. With flexibility comes opportunity — the opportunity to be happier, find meaningful pursuits and even make more money. (Stay tuned. I have a whole section about making it rain.)

"I don't have massive retirement savings."

The reality is that we're in post-secondary school longer and having children later (who will then live with us into infinity). We're juggling a lot more competing money priorities in our adulthood than previous generations did. In addition to carrying bigger mortgages, trying to find stable work and paying off student debt, some of us are supporting aging parents and raiding savings for fertility treatments. And trying to keep up with the Joneses on social media.

We don't always get to the goals we've set for ourselves, especially the all-important building of the retirement nest egg. But don't despair. We'll be getting into some smart strategies to help you make up for lost time.

These tough modern realities are not your fault. Shannon Lee Simmons, a financial planner and author of *Worry-Free Money*, says we need to make lemonade out of financial lemons. Financial lemons are things that are out of your control: money exploits that didn't work out, market crashes, rising interest rates, exploding (or crashing) house prices, the increase of part-time precarious work. "We need to take those lemons and still make a life for ourselves," she told me.

So worry less about where you think you're supposed to be. You're here. Let's plan where you want to go.

ARE YOU READY TO BE THE KING OR QUEEN OF YOUR OWN CASTLE?

Buying a house will be one of the largest purchases in your life. It deserves your deep thoughts. So hem and haw away. However, if you're agonizing over the decision, let me help you by answering some of your most likely questions as a first-time homebuyer.

1. Am I financially ready to be a homeowner?

Ask yourself, "Am I ready to commit?" Look at your lifestyle. Do you have stable income and can you plant roots for a few years? Buying and selling your house isn't an easy feat, and it costs money to buy real estate, including lawyer and realtor fees, home appraisal fees, taxes and moving costs. These closing costs are paid above and beyond the value of the home and range between 1.5% to 4% of the selling price.

Next, crunch some numbers to determine if you can afford the home you want. Your monthly housing costs (mortgage payments, taxes, heating, condo fees, home insurance, etc.) shouldn't be more than 32% of your gross monthly income. Use mortgage payment calculators. Ask other homeowners how much owning their homes cost. And don't forget to add in the closing costs.

2. How the heck do I amass a down payment?

If you've already begged your mom and dad and came up empty, it's going to take sacrifice and hustle. See if your parents will allow you to move home temporarily or if you can downgrade your living expenses, for example, by finding a roommate. Do what you can to boost your income and your savings, whether that's reducing spending or negotiating for a raise or working that side hustle.

3. Should I wait and save up 20% for a down payment?

Buyers who put down less than 20% must purchase mortgage default insurance in Canada or private mortgage insurance (PMI) in the U.S.; they also may qualify to borrow less. So if you're in an affordable housing market, aim for 20%. You won't have to pay for mortgage insurance and your monthly payments will be lower. That being said, you can put down less than 20%. Sixty-one percent of first-time homebuyers in America put down 6% or less in 2017, according to the National Association of Realtors. A smaller down payment means more liquid cash for your other priorities, and it allows you to get into the housing market sooner.

4. A starter castle in my city is way too expensive. Now what?

Your castle doesn't have to be a detached house in the city. Manage your expectations. Consider different types of homes. I started with a condo and then opted for a townhouse when Mofo and I got married. We also bought our house in the burbs versus the city core. I know people who have bought with family or friends. I know people who bought homes with rental units to offset costs. Be open-minded. Or keep renting, which can work too.

YOUR HAPPY MONEY TO-DO LIST

- Identify your worst-case financial scenario. How would you handle it? What do you have in your personal toolkit and in terms of support? Write out a plan in case of emergency.
- Challenge every single one of your negative thoughts and ask yourself, "Is this thought helpful or not?" Question your unhelpful thoughts. Ask, "Can I absolutely know if this thought is true? Have I had experiences that show this thought isn't always true? If someone I loved had this thought, what would I tell them? Who would I be without this thought?"

MONEY TALKS

- What is your biggest money worry?
- Name a money hang-up or fear. Is it founded? Does it have any truth?
- If you think you're "behind" in the money game, what benchmarks are you using? What positive benchmarks have you hit?

7
YOUR DEFAULT SETTINGS

When I was young, I tackled trick-or-treating with tenacity and strategy. I plotted a map for maximum door knocking and allowed for a mid-evening candy drop-off to reduce weight. I cut across lawns to save time. I brought my manners and my jokes to the door and then sprinted off. I would've donned a new mask and doubled back to the houses that gave chips if my dad would've let me. At home, I'd lay the loot out and sort it in order of preference and expiration (because back then, we'd eat anything including the cling-wrapped brownie). I'd make my haul last until the following October 31.

Even as a kid, I was a planner and into spreading out the joy. Were you like me? Or were you like Mofo, hoovering your candy within the week?

When it comes to how we approach our money, some of our behaviours and habits are innate while others were learned. To be happy with your money, you need to understand what your default is and how you feel about spending, saving and risk.

Know you

Scott and Bethany Palmer, co-authors of *The 5 Money Personalities*, say our money tendencies are baked into us at birth. "We are totally convinced with all of the research that we've done that your money personalities are cooked into you," Bethany Palmer told me. They identified five money personalities:

1. **Saver:** You take pleasure in saving, in discounts, in spreadsheets, in being frugal.
2. **Spender:** You have no problem parting with your cash.
3. **Risk taker:** You're a gambler. Driven by optimism, you like the thrill of the chase.
4. **Security seeker:** You're risk averse. Financial security and planning are your number one and two concerns.
5. **Flyer:** You fly by the seat of your pants and don't think too much about money. Often, relationships are more important to you than money.

Palmer says people are often a combination of two of these traits (a primary and secondary) and many times those traits can be opposing forces.

"We knew our kids' money personalities at ages three and four. The way you can tell is the way they handle Halloween candy," Palmer says. "A saver is going to want to save all of their candy. A spender is going to want to eat it all. A risk taker is going to want to trade it. A flyer could care less and give it all away. A security seeker is going to make their candy last a year."

In addition to our innate money habits, we come from different families and histories and will inevitably learn about money from those influences. My dad meticulously plans our family finances and prizes security. He reads the fine print. He doesn't take risks. He fretted about my going to Taiwan because I was risking my full-time stable job (stability in journalism, ha!). Meanwhile, he is generous with money, and he will not scrimp on things that he enjoys. I remember an argument that my parents once had because my father bought the expensive toilet paper, and my mom deemed it to be a waste. I vividly recall the anger and the declaration of what my dad's butt deserved.

Conversely, my mom shops for sport. But she needs sales like she needs air. She will spend four hours in one store, looking for the best deal, and she considers her time well spent because she found a purse for 90% off. She'll do anything to save money. She is infinitely creative — sewing clothing, bedding, upholstery, anything — to get beautiful things for less.

I am a sum of all of these parental parts.

Like my dad, it actually hurts me to gamble. I once received a free $10 voucher at a media event to bet on a horse race. Rather than lose (or win), I cashed out and spent the $10 on poutine for my best friend. And like my mom, I get off on discounts. I'll eat the expired jam to save a few bucks, and I spite my ass with construction-paper-like tissue.

If you're a security seeker, what will make you happy

is putting money aside for your priorities. But don't get so caught up in making sure that every plan is safe that you don't act and you say "no" to opportunities. If you're a flyer, you're content and you're not motivated by money, but as a grown-up, you need to think about money (you need to file taxes!) and looking up in the clouds could result in your falling into a money hole.

You have to know you. Then you have to work with that.

"Knowing your two money personalities and how they work together gives you clarity about your past; it gives you clarity about your present because you can think clearly about how to approach your money decisions and it gives you direction for your future," Palmer says.

Too cheap for your own good

Some of you are uber frugal. Even though that description sounds wonderful, like a smart, minimalist IKEA shelf, it might mean you are robbing yourself of joy by not investing in other priorities or hurting your relationships by being cheap. For hardcore savers, spending can also come with unnecessary pain. Every time we pay, it's okay to feel a pinch, a sting, but not a cramp. We pay for a lot of things and if you fret every time, the surge of cortisol and other stress hormones through your body will have ill effects.

Here are a few tips to lighten the hit.

Every time you pay for something and you feel like crap, think of everyone who benefits from your purchase. If you're buying groceries, feel gratitude about taking care of your family. Feel happy about supporting farmers and workers in your community. Feel proud that you're buying from a mom-and-pop store or an ethical company. (Okay, if you're shopping somewhere that employs underpaid children, then

I can't help you with this.) Feed your brain some positivity. Announce in your mind (out loud if you have no shame), "This purchase is in line with my values."

Designate a fun fund you're comfortable spending each month that won't compromise your larger goals. (More on this in an upcoming chapter!)

Adopt an abundance mindset as opposed to a scarcity mindset when it comes to your money. My entrepreneur friend Christa announces, "There's more where that came from." With the scarcity mindset, you become tunnel-focused on what you don't have. You fixate on the short term because of your limited resources. The alternative is to approach things with an abundance mindset, the thought that the world is your oyster and there are enough opportunities, resources and successes out there for everyone. It builds confidence, which inspires your behaviour, opens you up to look for new money opportunities and encourages you to collaborate with others rather than compete. There's more where that came from, indeed.

How to avoid conscious uncoupling

Knowing yourself can help with both inner conflict and the conflict you experience with a partner. In a 2009 research study entitled "Fatal (Fiscal) Attraction," researchers found that financial opposites attract; however, this attraction is ultimately bad for marriages because spenders and savers experience conflict.

Money is an ongoing argument in our house. Mofo will accuse me of being the cheapest person in the country, and I will call him a spendaholic. He'll be downstairs, filling his man cave with toys (there are pinball machines and a personal infrared sauna in our basement), and I'll be upstairs, mending the hole in a $30 sweater. We just value different things. And that may never change. No matter how many times I recite this book in his ear while he sleeps.

But taken together, our positions make for balance: he's working on our happiness for today, and I'm setting up our happiness for the future. He knows that far from being cheap, I'm extremely generous with my time and money. And I know that he never spends money we don't have and always takes care of our financial priorities first. It takes a lot of compromise and open discussion to make money decisions. And 90% of the time, we manage to get through without resorting to criticism or name-calling. High-five, Mofo.

To avoid chucking all your partner's gadgets out into the street, here are six tips to win at money with your honey.

1. Find the right time to talk money. Arming yourself with the credit card bill and accosting your partner at the door when they walk in from work is not a good time. I know. I tried it. It did not go well. Sig Taylor, a marriage and family therapist, told me to connect first: "When you talk about money, you want to make sure that you're coming from a connected, loving place. If you're upset with each other or you're in conflict, talking about money is going to fuel the flame." Go out for dinner, go for a walk — then bust out the fiscal chat.

2. Ask about the family. Money meaning grows on family trees. Start a money conversation by asking how finances were handled in their family. And talk about what money means to you. Maybe his parents refused to pay for any activities when he was growing up, so now he splurges on hockey lessons and toys for your kids because he never wants them to feel that disappointment. Maybe she saw her parent struggle as a single mom, so now she can't bear to buy new shoes, even if hers have holes in the soles, because she has to endure like her mother did. When you understand where someone is coming from, it's easier to make allowances for them.

3. Recognize your differences. Remember the five money personalities? Which one is your partner? If you understand their financial DNA, you can begin to accept who they are at their core. And learn to speak their language while teaching them some words from yours.

4. Make a dream sandwich. To make it easier to swallow, slap the bit about savings in between slices of goals and dreams. Instead of saying, "Let's have a talk about our finances" (snore), try, "Let's have a talk about our goals and dreams." Let's say you want to go to Europe next summer. You'll talk about how to make that happen. If the discussion is tense — with a lot of "we're going to have to cut back" — diffuse it immediately by doing something fun.

5. Show gratitude regardless of who makes the bread. Resentment can arise regardless of who is the primary earner. Mofo made more money when I was on maternity leave. While he always called it "our money" and he appreciated my contribution to our team as a stay-at-home mom, I still started to feel insecure and guilty about my purchases. I needed time to settle in to my new role and to truly see my own value. Mofo helped with excessive gratitude (there's really no such thing).

6. Address the "D" word. No, not death. But it's just as taboo — debt. People view and manage debt in different ways: one spouse could be scrimping to pay off their credit cards while another spends, confident that it will be taken care of in time. If you're married, it doesn't really make sense for one person to be carrying a ton of credit card debt while the other hoards cash. You must have a talk. What caused your debt? How long did it take you to build up the debt? Does your partner want to help pay your debt? If your partner agrees to bail you out, maybe you can give something up to help, thus taking responsibility for the hole that's been created.

YOUR HAPPY MONEY TO-DO LIST

- Figure out your default money tendencies and question whether they steal from your happy bank (and actual bank). Brainstorm with your OHM tribe what you can do to balance your default.
- If you're in a relationship, identify your partner's money tendencies. Have a talk with them about your similarities and your differences (without resorting to name-calling).

MONEY TALKS

- How did your parents handle money? Do you identify with them?
- If you're in a relationship, what do you appreciate about your partner's money tendencies?

8
SORRY NOT SORRY

Here are three things I regret buying recently:

1. Nordic print tights from a mall kiosk that reveal my entire ass when I bend over. (Hey, manufacturers: People. Have. Butts.)
2. The Instant Pot. Yeah, I said it. I bought it because I suffered from FOMO, and I've used it once.
3. A massage membership. Haven't been in eight months but still paying every month for a massage that I hope to enjoy now that this book is finished!

Quick: name something you regret recently buying. Despite the warrior cry of "no regrets," many of us feel pretty crappy about our spending. Reports on consumer regret often land in my inbox. Shopping vices. Dream home purchases. "Almost half of Americans have buyer's remorse about their house," reads one headline. "More than half of Canada's millennial homeowners want to sell their home because the cost of housing is making them cash poor," reads another article. Meanwhile, Canadians aged 18 to 29 are twice as likely as those over 50 to cite spending money on drinks and dinners as a regret.

I'm going to dwell on this as long as I think *you* should. The only way that your shame, guilt and regret will serve you is if it mobilizes you to act. Accept, acknowledge, look for the lesson in your error and move on.

Some purchases are a sunk cost. Economists and behavioural scientists use the term "sunk cost fallacy" to describe how the more money, time and effort we invest in something, the harder it is to give up on it.

Here are some examples from my life:

"Oh my God. This is the worst movie ever. But I've already watched a quarter of it, and I paid for VIP seating. I'll just suffer through for two more hours or I'll have wasted my money."

"*Ugh*. This tastes like someone made a burrito with decaying skunk meat. I'd throw it away, but my mom told me not to waste food. I'd return it for a refund, but I'm already at home."

Don't let that crappy purchase rob you of any more time or joy. Put down the burrito.

Underthinking leads to regret

Do you have stuff in your house with its price tag still on or that's never been used? I've wasted money on so much junk over the years — memorabilia, gadgets, clothing, designer fire extinguishers (maybe not the last one). Buying on auto-pilot — seeing something and purchasing it on a whim — is how Mofo gets in trouble online. Sometimes we put no thought into spending money. We might be temporarily pleased, but then we realize that was just a layover on the way to Regretsville.

If you don't take a moment before and after buying something to consider it in your life, so much is wasted. As personal development coach Nova Browning Rutherford says, if you buy more than you need, if you buy and don't use, you're not honouring the time that it took for someone to create that product, and you're not honouring the time and effort that you put into making the money to earn it. I like to think of the number of hours it took my teenage self to earn something. That's when I first learned the value of a dollar — working for minimum wage ($6 at the time) pouring meat out of a bag and squirting sour cream into tacos.

Plus you're missing out on so much joy if you're not even pausing to appreciate things. We have the ability to buy something with one click or the tap of plastic, but we need to create more time to breathe and think. We need to be more mindful with our purchases.

I have a 24-hour waiting period for purchases; I'll put something on hold or leave it in my online shopping basket. I'll take a picture of something I want to buy and send it through WhatsApp to my OHM tribe for consideration. We need time to process our choices. When we make choices, we use an area of the brain behind our brows. ("If I buy this amazingness now, I'll feel so happy.") But when we are considering more abstract consequences, we need another area of the brain near the left temple to help. ("If

I buy this amazingness now, what will this mean for my retirement savings down the road?")

We need time to let our brains work, to let that second area light up and activate self-control. We need to take a moment to consider the ramifications of our spending on our goals. What will it mean to be paying this item off for the next six months? What could we have spent this $1,000 on instead?

Delete your credit card information from your browser so that you have to put it in every time you go to buy something online. Take a beat to remember if there's something else worth waiting for instead.

During your pre-buy think-a-thon, consider two things to cut down on regret: is your purchase an experience or is your purchase unique? You are much less likely to regret buying an experience than regret buying stuff, says a paper in the 2012 issue of the *Journal of Personality and Social Psychology*. Remember experiences are often unique and incomparable. But your new phone can be compared to the many, many models already available (and the new ones just around the corner). In a separate experiment, researchers at Cornell University asked people to imagine buying an object that was common (a dresser at the mall) or unique (an antique dresser at an estate sale); people were much more likely to regret buying the mall dresser.

When I've taken the time to think, I'm less likely to make choices I regret or that are counter to my goals.

Overthinking still leads to regret

On the flip side, we expend a lot of effort rationalizing decisions in order to avoid regret. We're very persuasive when it comes to selling something to ourselves. When you're about to spend, especially money you don't have, how do you justify it?

- It's a once in a lifetime chance.
- This will change my life.
- I got a promotion, so I deserve this.
- My best friend is getting married and being in a wedding party makes relationships stronger. Melissa, you said to spend money on experiences and relationships, so I'm going to put the dress, the gifts, the shower and the Vegas bachelorette on my credit card and spend the next few years paying back the $3,000. Charge it!

Okay, let's be honest about what we're really buying at times. Are you buying payback from the revenge store? ("My ex will regret everything once he sees me in this.") Are you trying to make a deposit in the self-esteem bank? ("Screw Money Worries B-Gone. This $250 face cream has pond algae in it to smooth my crow's feet.") Are you trying to buy belonging? ("I can't afford this, but everyone here would appreciate me picking up the tab.")

When I was younger, my brain was a courtroom and I had an aggressive lawyer arguing that my wants were really needs. I needed to buy this blazer to impress at a job interview. I needed to buy the most expensive blender because it would kick-start a life of healthy smoothies. If your brain starts telling you, "If I don't buy this, then . . . ," that's the lawyer talking. If I don't buy this gym membership, I'm not going to be a sexy beast by summer. If I don't buy this for my family, they won't love me anymore; in fact, no one will.

Your lawyer is a big bullshitter.

In the coming chapters, I'll give you some tips on how to build a plan to avoid all of this back-and-forth and how to spend and save guilt-free. For now, I'd just suggest that you simplify your inner monologue to really stave off regret. Before I spend, my inner Judge Judy bangs the gavel to shush the courtroom and asks, "Is the way that I am spending my money in line with my values?"

If spending time with your parents who are out of town is important to you, maybe you can divert some of your funds from online shopping to your travel budget. If owning a home one day is important to you, where in your budget can you draw that money from? I'll help you identify what you value in another chapter.

I can't guarantee that you'll make the right decisions when you're faced with the question, but at least ask. When I was in Taiwan, I didn't have the funds to attend a best friend's destination wedding, and I chose not to go. To this day, I regret it. But we're closer today than we've ever been, so I just experience FOMO in flashbacks. One purchase, one anything really, will never decide everything.

Retail therapy leads to . . . yep, you got it, regret
Some of us enjoy a glass of wine with dinner. Some drink the wine to forget.

A little bit of shopping is normal. But maybe afterwards, the pain returns with its friends regret and self-loathing. Maybe you have to hide your bills and shopping bags from your roommate or spouse. Maybe you're constantly returning things (thank goodness for extended and flexible return policies). A report in the 2006 *American Journal of Psychiatry* estimates that roughly 5.8% of the U.S. population suffers from compulsive buying disorder. In 2013, *Friday Night Lights* author Buzz Bissinger wrote in *GQ* that he spent $587,412.97 on designer clothes in three years before going to rehab for his shopaholism.

Binge-spending to counter pain turns toxic. While you tackle the behaviour, also focus on the cause. If you have a spending habit, what triggers it? Reflect on times that you overspent. Was it after a fight with your parents? Were you bored? Stressed at work? When faced with this trigger in the future, is there something else that you can do to find comfort or reward yourself?

When you feel the urge, could you grab your phone instead of your wallet and call or text a friend? (Much like a former smoker reaches for vapes or gum instead of a cigarette.) If you tend to splurge on food and shopping on Fridays after work to decompress, could you schedule something else at 5 p.m., such as a class or a regular hike with a pal?

Find support for your abstinence; you don't have to go it alone.

No regrets

When I was in my early 20s, I'd announce that I lived life with no regrets. But now I think, "Girl, you hadn't had enough time to build up regrets." This is life. You can't learn or grow if everything has always gone your way or if you haven't made bad decisions. We regret not saving enough. We regret getting into debt. We regret trusting our friend with that investment. We regret not buying that condo 10 years ago, because now it's worth a bagillion dollars.

Every single time Mofo and I drive by a particular downtown waterfront property, we lament giving up an opportunity to buy it when it was dirt cheap. But we were young, and we made choices in that moment based on the knowledge and experience that we had. And I won't blame 21-year-old me for my present disappointments. I'm a big girl now. I can turn grains of regret into pearls of wisdom.

What would've been? Well, it never was and will never be. Time to let it go. Wherever you are in life right now, this too will change. You can look back at your choices and decide that going forward, you will choose differently. That's a wonderful gift. You'll never force-feed yourself a skunk-meat burrito again. You're welcome.

YOUR HAPPY MONEY TO-DO LIST

- Institute a waiting period before purchases. You need time to consider how to use your hard-earned money. (If it took you two hours to make the money to buy something, maybe at least have a two-hour waiting period before buying that thing.)
- Think about your discretionary purchases from the last week. How did you justify those buys?
- When you spend money poorly, don't hang on to it. Don't seethe with regret. You also bought a lesson. Learn and move on.

MONEY TALKS

- Play devil's advocate and argue why you may not have needed your last big purchase or how you could have compromised on it.
- What is one of your biggest money regrets? What is the lesson there? How can you now adapt?
- Would you buy an amazing jacket for $144? Would you work 24 hours making tacos and burritos to get it?

FEEL LIKE A MILLION BUCKS
(FOR FREE)

Don't get rich to get happy. Get happy first.

9
TRAIN YOUR HAPPY NINJA

I met Sean Cooper in 2014 when I interviewed him for a story with the headline "How this man plans to be mortgage free by age 31."

Sean was a 29-year-old pension analyst. He was $130,000 away from paying off his $425,000 three-bedroom bungalow in Toronto, without money from parents or the lotto. He lived in the basement and listened to his tenants thumping around upstairs.

We toured his unit, a museum of pre-owned and gifted furniture and items: his mother's brown couch, her cast-off floral pictures over his fireplace, a white dining set with puffy, lime chairs with black wheels on the legs. He planned to replace them, he said.

In his kitchen, puffed-out Ziploc bags rested upside down along the back of his sink like a string of lanterns because he washed and reused his sandwich bags. "Doesn't everyone do that?" he said earnestly.

His entire existence centred on his determination to achieve his mortgage-busting goal.

He woke up at 5 a.m. sometimes to write articles for extra cash on top of his $50,000 salary, and on the weekends, he worked at a grocery store. He once blogged about his meal plans, spending only $100 a month on groceries, eating meals that cost $1 to $2, consisting of rice cakes, almonds, water and a bagel for lunch or Kraft Dinner and frozen vegetables for dinner.

I looked around his home and I listened to him, and from under a veil of my own biases and hang-ups, I just couldn't relate to his lifestyle.

When the article was published, some readers felt the same and responded with hateful, douchebag comments as is the internet's wont. They commented on his austerity, his lack of fun, his prospects for sex. They were trying to tell him what would make him happy.

Sean told me that those comments had stung. But he stuck with his plan, and I admire his determination and his focus. I am, by no means, a slacker. But Sean had tenacity to an extreme. You can judge him all you want, but Sean was happy.

On a scale of one to ten, when he was paying off his mortgage, he said he was an eight. He was happiest the day that he stood in front of cameras surrounded by friends and media, wearing a suit and bowtie and lighting his mortgage papers on fire. He wrote a book, aptly entitled *Burn Your Mortgage*.

Since paying off his mortgage, Sean says, "It's been a bit of a letdown." He ranks his happiness now at a five.

But he won. He achieved. Here is Sean, whose net worth is an amazing half a million dollars (at least) in his early 30s, entirely built from his grit. But now he's dissatisfied. (The same thing happens to Oscar-winning actors and actresses, a celebrity psychologist once told me: they find themselves depressed after the win.)

Why? Maybe because Sean had staked his happiness on owning a structure of concrete, bricks and wood. Maybe because he became a man without a dream after that mortgage was paid off. Before, he knew what motivated him to get up every morning. Every minute of his time spent, every dollar that he earned, it had a purpose. He knew what motivated his happiness, and it didn't matter what others said should motivate him or what society said should make him happy. In the face of haters, he did something that fulfilled him. And it was all good until he stopped doing it.

Our external world — and what we buy or save — is not predictive of long-term happiness. Only 10% of your happiness is predicted by the outside world, psychologist Shawn Achor says. The way our brain processes the world and our outlook predicts 90% of our happiness.

Yet we put all of our stock in external things. First, we're collectors. We like to count things. We judge our worth by how much we make, how much we have in the bank, by the square footage of our homes, by the inches of our television. It's harder to quantify being a good dad or a loyal friend.

"We have been seduced into thinking that we can measure the value of our lives by our net worth. Yet if you look at the empirical evidence, people who make $5 million a year are only incrementally happier than blue-collar workers," Robin

Sharma, author of *The Monk Who Sold His Ferrari*, once told me in an interview. "I've worked with billionaires as a leadership coach–business advisor, and many of them are the most unhappy and empty people you've ever met. Why? Because they have a lot of money, and they don't have much else."

How do we retrain our brains that are so obsessed with material happiness and monetary worth? How do we turn ourselves into more positive people so we don't need to fill a void by buying? Practice. We have to boost our inner sense of joy. Positive emotions are magical: according to research, they have the power to do everything from lowering your stress to strengthening your immune system.

This may sound like a Deepak Chopra blog post, but stay with me. Experts in positive psychology often talk about your happiness set point. It's innate. You usually fall within a range on a set spectrum, regardless of what happens. Whether you win the lottery or break up with the love of your life, you'll reach extremes of emotions but often return to your set point. Yet there are things that we can do to bump our happiness set point.

At the height of Mofo's illness, my best friend and I were in a coffee shop where I was recapping the previous night, which had been particularly traumatic. Before parting ways, she asked me to rate my happiness in life on a scale of one to ten.

"Seven," I said without hesitation.

"Oh my God. If your life is a seven, then mine must be a 12," she blurted.

Humans by nature are optimistic. We overestimate the longevity of our marriages and underestimate the chances of getting cancer. Ninety percent of us think that we're above average drivers (even my mother-in-law — I love her, but she thinks other drivers are constantly waving at her with just one finger). But we can be even more positive. Even people like me, who used to be a Debbie Downer (Miserable Missy? Melissa Melancholia?).

Your mission, should you choose to accept it

Researchers say that people who feel that life has meaning or purpose report less anxiety, pain and stress. So, what gives you the sense that your day was worth it?

Figuring out what is important to you will help you make priorities. Then try to rearrange your day or make tweaks to do more life-affirming things. At the least, remind yourself regularly of your greater mission. If your mission is to make the best life for your husband and kids and you're working overtime to buy a family home, change your phone screensaver to a photo of your family. If you feel happiest being a community mobilizer, prioritize your weekends to do more of that and accept that other areas of life will be less than perfect.

When Mofo and I are busiest, piles of laundry will appear as if giant ants are colonizing our floors; I'll walk around the bathroom with horror like I'm Sigourney Weaver tiptoeing around giant eggs in the queen alien's lair. "It would be easier to unleash a flame thrower on the piles and just wear garbage bags," I think.

But I tell myself, "Relax. It's okay. I can't do it all. My resources are elsewhere."

Take time for yourself to work on your mind, your body and your emotional life. And while it's great to take care of yourself and your family, Sharma says, what makes life matter is living for a cause that's larger than yourself. "You don't have to be a Steve Jobs or a Nelson Mandela. You can be an ordinary person who says I'm going to do my part to uplift people, take care of the environment and take care of my community."

My great grandfathers came to Canada from China and started businesses in small prairie towns. They left behind their wives to raise children and even grandchildren on their own through adversity and war. Decades later, my mother's family and my father's family would come together in one building — the Shanghai restaurant, one of the first Chinese restaurants in Winnipeg's Chinatown. In the '50s, the lineups would start at its hulking neon-red sign and snake around the building, even in winter.

Many of my 16 cousins and I grew up there. I ran around steel serving carts, rattling with plates of glistening beef and battered shrimp. I stole fortune cookies and dipped my fingers in sweet and sour sauce so bright red that it looked radioactive. My uncles started there as teenagers and worked every day and night, including weekends and holidays. My father worked his nine-to-five Monday to Friday, and then every weekend and Christmas Eve and New Year's Eve, he also worked at the restaurant.

The money that was earned through that restaurant, my grandfather donated back to the Chinese community. In the 1980s, he helped revitalize Winnipeg's Chinatown; the structural plans for a new Chinese culture centre served as my colouring books as a toddler (sorry, Gung Gung).

Just before the restaurant closed after 70 years of business, before the building was razed to rubble, Winnipeggers who had been coming for 10, 20, 30 years poured through the doors for one last bite; they had created so many memories there, and they took menus and matchbooks as souvenirs. That place, and what they put into it, will live forever in so many of us. It gave my family a foundation on which to grow. We are its enduring legacy.

So, if you ever think about your days, your work — whatever it may be, however simple or backbreaking or stressful — and the fruits of your labour and bemoan that it's all for nothing, look again. Are you giving your family a better chance at this beautiful life? Are you helping strangers in the smallest way? Are you fulfilling a service to your community? We yearn for meaning. Sometimes it can be found by looking a little closer at what you're already doing.

Sean Cooper is finding his joy again. He's been travelling and, most importantly, he's devoted himself to educating others about home ownership and finances.

Enough is a feast

As soon as I am conscious in the morning, when I'm stopped at a red light, before I slip into slumber, when I'm feeling annoyed with Mofo or my boss or my frenemy, I count my blessings. In any given moment, I try to come up with at least three new things to be grateful for.

Right now:

- I am grateful that I have knowledge to share.
- I am grateful that you've picked up this book.
- I am really grateful that you can't see my happy dance, which is all upper body and looks as if I'm karate chopping an imaginary massage client.

Your turn.

Many studies have concluded that cultivating gratitude in daily life affects our brains and increases our happiness. Researchers at Indiana University recruited adults who were reporting low levels of mental health and asked some of them to write a letter of a gratitude each week for three weeks. Three months later, fMRI scans revealed that their brains reacted differently than the brains of those who had not done the exercise, revealing a potential lasting effect.

Silent appreciation has superpowers — it can make you feel more positive, improve health, help you deal with challenges and strengthen relationships. In one study, a group of people who recorded daily gratitude for 10 weeks were happier, exercised more and had fewer visits to the doctor than those who wrote about daily irritations. Managers who say thank you to their employees may find workers feel motivated to work harder.

We have to be more grateful for all things — material and intangible. We can be grateful for our memories, our today and our future opportunities. We can be grateful for others.

On International Women's Day, I wrote personal thank-you messages to 50 women who have made a difference in my life. I have gratitude partnerships with friends where we have to report to each other on a regular basis. Then I'll print them gratitude books filled with their responses. I spontaneously ask others about what they appreciate. If you follow me on Instagram, you may have received one of those messages: "Quick, tell me something you're grateful for!"

Not surprisingly, 90% of what I appreciate and what others tell me is immaterial. Sure, I'm grateful that we have the money for a manual reel lawn mower that Mofo bought on Amazon after seeing Don Draper grate his grass with one on *Mad Men*. But I'm actually more grateful that I have the health and the strength to shove that thing across our bumpy yard.

Highlight your highlights

Researchers at the University of Pennsylvania tested a number of exercises aimed at boosting happiness:

- Delivering a letter of gratitude
- Reflecting on a time when you were at your best
- Listing three good things in your life
- Using your strengths in a new way

Which do you think had the most powerful and lasting effects on happiness? The latter two exercises made people happier (and less depressed) up to six months later.

The researchers who worked on these exercises asked participants to fill out a questionnaire at AuthenticHappiness.org to identify their character strengths. Then they were asked to use these strengths every day for a week in a way that they've never done before. After answering all 240 questions, I learned that my top strengths include curiosity, diligence and playfulness. That week, I asked the barista at my regular coffee shop about her life in Syria, I wrote 3,000 words in one sitting for this book, and I came up with two very catchy new nicknames to replace Negatron (high-five to myself for using alliteration).

As for the other exercise, try this: every night this week, write down three things that went well that day and their causes. Share them with your partner. Email them to your Oh Happy Money tribe. Mofo and I ask each other at the end of every day, "What was your highlight?" It's like putting a knot on the thread that is our day, so that it doesn't just pull through without any moments to remember. And it's usually something our son said or did — fed our fish his toast, manned an imaginary ice-cream truck where we just couldn't get enough of his pronunciation. ("What are you selling, sweetie?" "Ass cream. Do you want ass cream?")

According to Rick Hanson, a neuropsychologist and author of *Hardwiring Happiness,* the longer you focus on a positive thing, the more you linger on a happy moment, the more likely your brain will create a neural pathway for more positivity. Unfortunately, we tend to obsess more over negative thoughts. (How many times has my editor said a bunch of nice things about my story but all I remember is the one criticism?) It's an evolutionary gift since it was more important to our survival to remember that a sabre-toothed cat lived around the bend than to remember that there were tasty nuts in the same area. Our brain is trying to keep us alive — but not necessarily happier. But we can change that.

The best things in life are free

Nothing beats a nap. British researchers from the University of Hertfordshire in 2017 found a link between happiness and short naps (under 30 minutes). They call the smiley feelings after a brief daytime snooze "nappiness." Free activities such as napping, walking and reading have a profound impact on our well-being, according to multiple studies. And they're so often overlooked.

Make a list of some of the simpler things that give you pleasure — and enjoy one before the end of the day. For inspiration, take this story about palliative pediatrician Alastair McAlpine. In 2018, he asked his young patients what they had enjoyed in life and what gave it meaning. They loved spending time with loved ones, and they loved laughing. They cherished inspiring stories and books. They loved kind people and remembered acts of kindness. "The last words I heard from one little girl were, 'Thank you for holding my hand when I was scared,'" Dr. McAlpine wrote in the *Guardian*. He shared the key takeaways on Twitter: "Be kind. Read more books. Spend time with your family. Crack jokes. Go to the beach. Hug your dog. Tell that special person you love them . . . and eat ice cream."

YOUR HAPPY MONEY TO-DO LIST

- Make gratitude a deliberate part of your day. I use apps (Bliss for Android) and journals (The Five-Minute Journal) that prompt gratitude. Connect with me on Twitter or Instagram (@lisleong) and tell me what you're grateful for, and I'll tell you what I'm grateful for.
- Visit AuthenticHappiness.org. It's free, but you'll need to set up a username and password. You can take a whole bunch of questionnaires, but use the VIA Survey of Character Strengths to identify your superpowers and then put them to new and better use.
- Every night this week, write down three things that went well in the day and how each happened.

MONEY TALKS

- What fulfills you? What gives you the sense that your day was worth it? Are you spending your money and time here?
- How many days out of 100 would you say that you're happy? What causes your unhappy days? What can you do to change that? What can you do to change that for someone you care about?

- Name someone who contributes to society in a way that you admire. How can you use your strengths to do something similar?

10
INVOKE THE DOLLAR LAMA

After Mofo's mind fractured in 2014, he was referred to a program for meditation at a hospital. Psychiatrists said that they were having as much success treating mental illnesses, including depression and anxiety, with meditation as they were with pills.

Before this, being neither religious nor spiritual, I had associated meditation with yogis and monks and hippies. I remember feeling annoyed when a speaker at a professional conference once asked the audience to join her in a short meditation, and I used that two minutes to create a grocery list. I remember a work colleague explaining Chakra meditation and psychic energy, and my mind started playing the theme song to *The X-Files* over her voice.

But now I know meditation is exercise for your brain, burpees to beef up your grey matter. Thousands of studies suggest positive benefits to meditation. A whole slough of brain-scanning studies show that meditation can alter the brain. They've put everyone from meditating monks to beginners taking an eight-week mindfulness course into fMRI machines and watched the brain change. A team at Harvard University in 2011 found that mindfulness meditation increases grey matter in parts of the brain associated with learning, remembering, regulating emotions, taking perspective and processing thoughts in relation to self. Corporations such as Procter & Gamble and Google and organizations like the United States Marine Corps offer meditation classes for their staff and members. An elementary school in Baltimore uses meditation instead of detention.

If your expression is the thinking face emoji, read on. Your brain will thank you.

Your antidote to mindlessness

One of the most popular types of meditation is mindfulness meditation. A lot of us think of meditation as a state of clear-minded enlightenment, but for most of us mere mortals, mindfulness is just paying attention to the moment. Here are the basics, which you can try for as little as a minute.

1. Most people sit, but meditation can also be done walking, standing or lying down. No need to go all human pretzel or buy a fancy meditation cushion.
2. Try to pay attention to your breath (repeat "in, out" or count your breaths if it helps you focus) or the sounds around you or the feel of your body.

3. When your mind wanders (it will), bring it back to whatever you were focused on. Don't worry if you get distracted and have to keep starting again. That's normal. In fact, continually bringing your attention back to the moment *is* the exercise. Try not to judge yourself for getting distracted or for any of your thoughts.

If this really isn't for you, you can achieve mindfulness without formal meditation or yoga. Ellen Langer, a social psychologist at Harvard University, defines it as "the simple process of actively noticing things." It's a shortcut to being alive to the present moment. Using data from thousands of people, Harvard psychologist Matthew Killingsworth determined that we are happiest when we are experiencing the present moment instead of letting our minds wander. So, really listening to your kid tell you a story versus mm-hmm'ing and checking emails. Eating and tasting your lunch versus shovelling it into your face hole on a 30-minute break while thinking about your next meeting. Focusing on your running or your gardening or folding the laundry.

When I was in Taiwan, I lived entirely in the moment. I saw everything. I felt everything. During typhoons, fat droplets exploded on my face like minuscule water balloons, and cockroaches that had scrambled up from flooded sewers snapped like firecrackers under my shoes. During heat waves, I'd suck in the soupy air and linger in slivers of shade made by lamp posts. I journalled and I reflected. I remember the days vividly because I'd never been more present.

My best friend, Kerry, who is one of the happiest people I know, practises mindfulness on a daily basis without recognizing it. She'll sit at her kitchen table and look out the window. She just sits. She'll observe the sway of the trees, the hop and flit of a bird. She'll sip her tea and notice the bump of the tea bag against her upper lip. And then it's off to the next thing. But this small exercise done many times in the day does magical things for her psyche. She feels more balanced, is better able to identify her thoughts and emotions and is thus more likely to analyze them before acting.

For me, the greatest benefit of practising mindfulness has been to help me to observe my thoughts. The first time someone told me to do that, I thought, "Huh? I see my thoughts all the time. What do you mean?" Dan Harris, ABC News journalist and author of *10% Happier*, imagines a waterfall — these are your thoughts — and mindfulness is the area behind the waterfall where you can safely stand and look at your urges, impulses and wants without getting swept up in them. In the beginning, to "see" my thoughts, I imagined that whatever popped into my mind ("Chartreuse is too nice of a name for that butt-ugly colour," "Zipper merge, people!") was enclosed in a thought bubble. The bubble would then move on, like I was turning to a new blank page in a book. It's helped me notice the non-stop mental diarrhea running through my mind. Mindfulness takes you off autopilot, which — let's be honest — is how we live a lot of our days. Think of when you drove to work and had no recollection of how you even got there. Or how you go into a store and mindlessly buy things.

Money expert Chantel Chapman teaches meditation to shopping addicts. She holds money and meditation seminars where her students do a 30-day meditation challenge for overspending. The challenge means that every day they must practise controlling the breath with alternate nostril breathing (they block their right nostril, inhale, hold and exhale seven times through the left). "With debt, we're on this hedonic hamster wheel," she says. "If you think of people who have addiction issues, they're trying to reduce pain in their lives, whether from trauma or stress, and they're using drugs or alcohol or sex or spending to increase pleasure — which then creates even more pain."

You don't need a shopping addiction to have mindfulness benefit your bank account. Steady meditation allows you to check out of the chaos, your Instagram feed and the crafty advertising telling you "because you're worth it." You'll note your thoughts a little more objectively and be aware of your feelings before simply reacting.

Here's an example of an automatic response in my brain: "Look, there's a toy my kid doesn't have. Buy it now to complete his collection." Now here's how my mindful brain processes this: "Look, there's a toy my kid doesn't have. Oh, I am recognizing my impulse to buy it. Well, he already has this dog in a firetruck, but his firetruck doesn't have a ladder and he loves ladders. Okay, I am recognizing that I'm now rationalizing why he needs it and how it would make him happy. But it's on sale . . ."

Even if I still buy the firefighting canine, I am more thoughtful about the purchase. This isn't a magic pill. It doesn't always work, judging by the number of heroic dog figurines we have around the home. But it gives me more of a fighting chance.

Mofo meditates regularly. He goes to a mindfulness class at a community centre. They go through a series of different exercises: body scan (where you focus your attention on your bits, from head to toe), a loving-kindness meditation (where you send your well-wishes to yourself and then to others), a raisin meditation (where you use all of your senses on, well, a raisin). I prefer finding pockets of time to be mindful and doing guided imagery meditations — perhaps the lazy woman's way to meditate. I click a YouTube link, and I listen to someone prompt me to imagine a beach or beautiful meadow or with questions. I fight the impulse to turn on the radio when waiting in a drive-thru, and I concentrate on the movement of my belly with my breathing. I'm adopting the mindfulness practices that I find meaningful to me. Each one is a single push-up for my brain. It makes me happy to know that I'm doing something to improve my best asset.

AN INTRODUCTION TO LOVING-KINDNESS (METTA) MEDITATION

Metta is the practice of sending well-wishes to yourself and others. A 2008 study published in the *Journal of Personality and Social Psychology* found that just seven weeks of practising this meditation boosted happiness and life satisfaction and decreased depression. More research has shown that it can reduce migraines and chronic pain and even slows aging. So, in addition to your anti-wrinkle facial massage routine, bust out the love and kindness. Here's how.

1. Sit and get comfy. Close your eyes. Take two or three deep breaths and exhale slowly. For a few minutes, feel or imagine your breath moving in and out of your body, through your nose, through your chest.

2. Start by sending well-wishes to yourself. That's right. You love you.

3. Mentally repeat, "May I be happy. May I be healthy. May I be safe and at ease."

4. As you say these phrases, imagine yourself and connect with any fuzzy feelings of warmth or love. If you don't feel warm fuzzies, don't sweat it. Feel good about wanting yourself to feel good. If you're not loving yourself today, picture yourself as a child at your most adorable.

5. Next bring to mind someone who loves you or who has loved you. Imagine them as vividly as possible.

6. Mentally repeat, "May you be happy. May you be healthy. May you be safe and at ease."

7. Start with someone easy, and as you build up the good vibes, you could progress to harder and harder people. For example:

   • A friend or family member or someone in your life who has cared about you.

   • A neutral person — someone you know but who you have no special feelings toward. Maybe your barista or Andy in the mailroom.

   • A person who you are having difficulty with. Yeah. Even that d-bag.

   • Everyone. Send warm wishes to everyone around you, in your neighbourhood, your country and throughout the world. They, like you, just want to be happy.

8. Take a deep breath. Note how you feel. Open your eyes.

YOUR HAPPY MONEY TO-DO LIST
- Practise mindfulness. Try it now. Sit and focus on your breath for one minute.
- Take it to the next level: sign up for a meditation course or download a mindfulness session or app. Mofo and I borrowed some audiobooks by Jon Kabat-Zinn from the library to start.

MONEY TALKS
- What are your feelings about meditation?
- Reflect on the last time that you were truly in the moment. What did that feel like?

11
INVEST IN BONDS

When I was 24, I flew to Hong Kong to do an investigative report on its foreign domestic workers. Among its population of 7.4 million are hundreds of thousands of women, mainly from the Philippines and Malaysia, working as nannies and personal care workers. I landed on a Sunday, their only day off, and the streets, squares and parks were teeming with women. They had set up stalls along the sidewalk, selling their wares. They spread mats and blankets on the grass and concrete, eating lunch, laughing, chatting. In private interviews, I spoke to women who had been separated from their families, their children, for decades in order to care for other families and other children. They endured long hours and, in some cases, abuse.

I spent a day at a shelter for nannies fleeing abuse. That day happened to be my birthday and my guide/translator knew. As I gathered my tape recorder and purse to leave, 25 women at the shelter filed into a living room, singing "Happy Birthday" and carrying a small cake.

I still get emotional thinking about their smiling faces as they belted out the song. They had very little in terms of possessions and opportunities and power. They were hurting (one young woman showed me the bright purple bruise on her thigh, in the shape of a rectangular can she'd been struck with). They didn't know me. They'd probably never see me again. And I had just spent hours asking them about their fears and their traumas.

But they had the power to be kind. They could do this one nice thing for a stranger. It will always remind me that even if I have nothing, I have it in me to be giving. I can always take the time and effort to connect with another human being.

Plus, being kind is also good for your self. Acts of kindness are scientifically proven to make you feel good. Do it regularly and your brain will become addicted to feeling good by making others feel good. "We scientists have found that doing a kindness produces the single most reliable momentary increase in well-being of any exercise we have tested," Martin Seligman writes in his book *Flourish*.

Start every day by sending a short email or text or tweet praising someone. I used to do this in the form of an email to a fellow journalist, telling them that I enjoyed their story and asking them why they're so much smarter than I am. Mow your neighbour's lawn. Choose a book from your library and lend it a friend who'll love it. Send someone a great photo of them.

Our brains become addicted to feeling good by making others feel good. If it's an automatic habit to hold doors open for strangers, find new ways to be considerate. It'll look good, but it'll feel better.

Human assets

My parents are avid but undiscerning cinephiles. We used to share a Netflix account until their terrible choice in movies threatened to destroy my marriage and family relations. Before Netflix introduced separate profiles, Mofo wanted to disavow all Leongs after his recommended titles category offered only straight-to-DVD rom coms and belief-suspending action films.

If you want to spend time with my mom and dad, you have to watch movies, possibly bad ones, and when I was in my 20s, I didn't want to do much of that. But over the years — and with some distance from the family home — I've come to watch not only the movie but my parents. They both talk during movies, as if they're watching the NBA finals and they're doing the live commentary.

"She can deflect bullets. What is the use of loading the gun?" my dad said, waving at the TV screen playing *Hansel & Gretel: Witch Hunters*.

"Waaaah! This is *The Walking Dead* on Viagra!" my mom exclaimed while we watched *World War Z*.

Recalling these times, two things are clear to me. One, I never want to hear my mom use the word "Viagra" in front of me again. Two, seeing my parents smile or laugh or get excited about silly movies fills me with joy.

In my son's first three years of life, I've taken him on a plane from Toronto to Winnipeg at least 12 times to visit them. The kiddo will sit with his Gung Gung in a folding camp chair on the driveway and watch the cars and trucks go by and it's perfect. I'm happy in the moment. And I'm happy today remembering it.

Palliative care nurse Bronnie Ware, who wrote *The Top Five Regrets of the Dying*, said, "People do want to get their financial affairs in order if possible. But it is not money or status that holds the true importance to them . . . It all comes down to love and relationships in the end."

I wish I could spend more time with my parents, who encouraged me to move out to Toronto to chase my dreams when I was 18. I wish I could've spent more time with my grandmother before she passed away. This woman who came to Canada and rode two buses every day, even in blizzard conditions, to work at a sewing factory for decades to give her family a better life. This woman who was one of the first people to love me and who continued to love me, even in my absence from home, even when I forgot to call her to say hello.

The more I focus on relationships, the more I want to make the most out of all of them.

In 1938, scientists began tracking the health of 268 Harvard University students. The study continues to this day and has provided insight into what leads to healthy and happy lives. No surprise: it's close relationships. Spending time with others made people happier on a day-to-day basis, protected them from life's downs and life's pains and helped delay the deterioration of the brain and body. "Many of our [study participants] when they were starting out as young adults really believed that fame and wealth and high achievement were what they need to go after to have a good life. But over and over these 75 years, the study has shown that the people who fared the best were the people who leaned into relationships with family, with friends, with community," psychiatrist Robert Waldinger, who is the director of the study, said in a famed TED Talk. "Good relationships keep us happier and healthier. Period."

Good relationships with parents in childhood often turned into good relationships in adulthood. Many of my friends work so much and spend so much time away from the kids (in the pursuit of more money and security for the kids) and I think of one of the top regrets of the dying reported by Ware: "I wish I hadn't worked so hard."

And what about the relationship that has the most influence on your happiness and your lifespan? Marriages with a lot of conflict are physical and mental poison, maybe worse than divorce, Waldinger says. The good news is that we have some control over the quality of our relationships. My husband and I started doing proactive counselling shortly after getting married to make sure we were prepared for the challenges ahead. Of all the fun communication exercises we did, none of them said anything about what to do when your husband ends up in a hospital's psychiatric wing.

During that time, my most valuable resources were people. The family who came to appointments, the friends who brought dinner, the acquaintances who revealed their own struggles. They were there for me, as I've tried to be for them over the years. Strengthen your army of people — by being a member of their army. If you know someone is struggling, reach out to them. (That includes caregivers and everyone affected — not just the individual who is suffering or sick.) As Sheryl Sandberg has suggested in her interviews about her book *Option B*, just show up. Instead of telling them, "If you need anything, call me," say, "I'm coming over with dinner. Is Chinese takeout okay?" Instead of saying, "I didn't know what to say so I wanted to give you space," ask them how they're doing today. When Emily McDowell was battling cancer, she says loved ones disappeared because they didn't know what to say. She created a greeting card line (including one that says, "Please let me be the first to punch the next person who tells you everything happens for a reason. I'm sorry you're going through this.") and co-authored the book *There Is No Good Card for This*. She suggests that you just keep things simple: be there to listen, call, text, check in and just show up. She also advises people to help in ways that come naturally: for example, if you love to cook, cook. But if you're a logistical whiz, maybe you'd be better organizing a cooking schedule for other friends and family. Your time and your care are priceless, and you might only realize that when you receive those things in return.

Mofo says everyone is my best friend — which is untrue. I have a spare kidney for exactly seven BFFs. These relationships have evolved over the years. (Really, I have to question any "friend" who supported my decision to dye my black hair blond in the early 2000s. And "friends" who let me go to a formal event dressed in a white pantsuit topped with a white hat, without any irony; I was going for a Céline Dion at the 1999 Oscars look but was told after the fact that I looked more like the man from the Del Monte fruit ads.)

But good friendships are elastic — sometimes close, sometimes stretched further, but always there. All still require effort and time. To have good friends, you have to *be* a good friend. To improve relationships, happiness guru Gretchen Rubin suggests that we try to offer warm hellos and goodbyes to our family, friends and co-workers. She emails her parents regular updates on her family's day-to-day life (with no obligation to reply) and reaches out to people to congratulate them or compliment them.

Research also shows that to boost relationship quality and satisfaction, do something new and interesting together. (Note to my own OHM tribe: once again, *no*, I am not interested in bungee jumping or any activity where gravity squeezes my innards toward my head like a toothpaste tube. I know extreme experiences like the dates on *The Bachelor* super-strengthen our bonds, but I've heard painting nights can be thrilling.)

What about people you unintentionally said goodbye to? In Ware's book, people wished they had stayed in touch with friends. They didn't have Facebook, but even these days, an annual birthday GIF on someone's wall doesn't replace seeing them face-to-face. (Fact: I just took a writing pause to invite my university roommate out for lunch.) A 2003 study in a leading psychotherapy journal showed that people who had face-to-face, rather than online, interactions felt more satisfied and closer to the other person.

Connecting with strangers also has benefits. I'm not talking about smiling at the subway manspreader, but treating the familiar characters and even passersby in your life like they're human beings lightens your day. I try to make eye contact with everyone I interact with — the cashier at the grocery store, the doorman at the office. I always know the names of the concierges where I live, the editorial assistants where I work, the baristas who regularly serve my drinks; it made me sad (and angry) when a concierge told me that I was one of the few people who said hi to him every day. We're sleepwalking through life and ignoring the most valuable thing about society: people. Maybe the next time you order something with free shipping, connect with the bonus human who arrives at your door to deliver it.

YOUR HAPPY MONEY TO-DO LIST

- Organize a date or friend night and do something different. Axe throwing. Board games. Enjoy.
- Learn (and remember) someone's name who you regularly see and one detail about their life. Then ask them about that detail on your second meeting. Or the next time you offer someone on the street a donation, ask their name.
- Ask a family member or friend what their favourite meal or chocolate treat is. Schedule a reminder in your calendar for a month from now to surprise them with it.
- Start every work shift with an act of kindness: a thank-you note, a compliment, a coffee for your office bestie.
- Reach out to someone you care about but have lost touch with.

MONEY TALKS

- Would you rather have a $100,000 salary but see your best friends once a month or a $50,000 salary and spend time together every week?
- If aliens blew up the world tomorrow, what would you regret?

12
EAT, PLAY, SNOOZE

I worked full throttle in my 20s. And when Negatron operates on max, she starts a self-destruct timer.

By 22, I had worked at three newspapers. Following that, I was among a handful of young journalists plucked from hundreds of applicants to participate in a lauded internship program at the country's largest newspaper. Walking every day into a sprawling newsroom, I felt the fear of failure like a knife pressed to my throat. So I turned off my mind, and I just ran.

Once, I got a phone call at dawn from my editor about a plane crash in Windsor. I rolled out of bed and rushed out the door to drive from Toronto. Near the end of my four-hour drive in a blizzard, the car ran out of windshield-washer fluid and the glass looked as if it had been painted with grey mud. Did I pull over because I couldn't see? Nope. I drove on the highway with my head out the window, subjecting myself to a road facial, the sleet exfoliating off layers of skin. I was desperate not to lose time, because every minute not on the ground was a minute I was missing out on a story.

Throughout my 20s, I kept making phone calls, and I kept knocking on doors. I sweated in my car on too many stakeouts, waiting to get a juicy quote from a smarmy politician, an alleged criminal, a disgraced businessman. I attended too many funerals for people I didn't know. I spoke to too many grieving families and victims of crime or disaster.

After a 10-hour workday, I'd still cling to my phone because there might be a call about my story. News to add. Rewrites to do. Points needing clarification. I changed the contact name and photo for the newsroom on my cellphone, so when an editor called, it would appear as a flower with the words "Happy Place." I still cringed.

I was on a string of contracts, so the threat of not having a job loomed over me. There was intense competition, even among colleagues. You wanted to be on the front page. And if you were on the front yesterday, that was so yesterday and so you needed to be on it again.

It wasn't always doom and gloom and stress and deadlines. There was incomparable adventure and travel. There were amazing interviews and people — scholars, heroes, royalty and celebrities. There was a wonderful sense of purpose and a duty to the public.

But in my late 20s, I started getting panic attacks. I would be at my desk or lying in bed and my heart would suddenly jackhammer as if I had just been sprinting and my breath would get trapped in my throat as if I was trying to draw it through a nipped straw. I saw a therapist through my work's employee assistance program, and she said it was a wonder that I hadn't experienced them before with the stress and pressure that I subjected myself to. Looking back, I had ignored signs of mental deterioration. I remember many times hiding at Kerry's house in tears because I was scared to go to work. I can recall that deep sense of dread that dug its nails into my body on a daily basis. But I thought that was the price of succeeding and the nature of this important work.

I had started Latin dancing to decompress soon after beginning an internship. I went salsa dancing almost every night — and then I started teaching and performing. I danced for hours, at least three times a week for more than a decade. If I had a tough day at work, I could literally shake it off and spin it away, like putting my mind on a wash cycle.

Therapists would later tell me that this was my physical meditation. And, more importantly, my powerful antidote to stress. I'm convinced Negatron would have blown all fuses without this musical and physical intervention.

We invest in our careers and in our pursuit of wealth, but we deprive our bodies. We need to invest more in our health, or all the bonds, stocks and vacation properties won't be of any use. To be happier, especially in the face of work and life pressures, we need to take better care of ourselves — and it needn't cost a lot of money.

Shake that booty

Medical researchers at Duke University have shown that 30 minutes of brisk exercise three times a week is as effective as drug therapy in relieving symptoms of major depression, and continued exercise reduces the chances of the depression returning. In a study of 156 patients, those who only took drugs had a relapse rate of 38%. Meanwhile, only 8% of the patients who only exercised saw their depression return. Following a mental health nurse's advice, Mofo took up walking with a friend as a salve for his anxiety.

Obviously, you don't have to be depressed to benefit from exercise. Exercise boosts your health, your brain power and your self-image. And this isn't an ad for pricey candlelit spin classes or a boutique gym membership (though a well-used gym membership might give you more joy for your buck than a well-used booth at the club with bottle service). There are a lot of ways that you can build up a sweat without working up a debt: walking or cycling to work, running, rounding up friends for pick-up basketball at a park. Your local community centre also offers fitness programming from yoga to swimming.

Salsa dancing at bars was almost always free. Then I volunteered to teach so I could do more of it for free. After that, I was paid $70 an hour for a private lesson or $100–$200 to perform at your wedding or corporate Christmas party.

So join me on the dance floor. Or, at the very least, take a lunch break and go for a walk.

Swipe right on the Sandman (and then put the phone down)

Our brains function better with sleep. We're better able to regulate our emotions; we feel more alert and less drowsy. Even small levels of sleep deprivation can chip away at our ability to be chipper. Seventeen to 19 hours without sleep is equivalent to blood alcohol content of 0.05 (driving over 0.08 is against the law), according to one 2000 Australian study. It's all the fog and none of the fun.

But if getting good sleep is one of your challenges, I understand your pain.

I know this struggle first-hand as Mofo and I have dealt with insomnia. Mine has been present for most of my life, lurking and reappearing here and there, like an alley cat. Some nights, I couldn't shut off the incessant ticker of thoughts, checklists, scenarios and memories running behind my closed eyes. I couldn't dial down the volume on some irritating ditty I had heard earlier in the day that would loop in surround sound in my mind at bedtime. Mofo's weapons-grade insomnia came after he tried to stop taking sleeping pills. He couldn't sleep for days.

In our household, sleep became an obsession. In our circles, "How'd you sleep?" replaced "How are you?" We checked my husband in to a sleep clinic to rule out sleep apnea. We flew to an Arizona health resort to see its director of sleep medicine. We downed warm milk, specialty teas and natural supplements. We tried hypnosis, acupuncture, flotation therapy. We kept sleep logs, adhered to consistent wake and sleep times and instituted a rigid bedtime regime that included dimmed lights, hushed voices, no digital screens and lavender-scented showers. My husband boarded up the windows with bristol board to eliminate any light and stuffed his ears with plugs to muffle any sound. Our home became a graveyard for pillows and mattresses because, like Goldilocks, we were on a quest for the ones that were just right.

I'm happy to report that our sleep has much improved (toddler notwithstanding). We're much happier when we feel rested. An extra hour of sleep for me means the difference between smiling through my kid's tantrums and locking myself in the car to unleash a tear-inducing scream.

But sometimes we sabotage our own sleep. We forgo sleep to work, to strive, to succeed and then wear it like a badge of honour. We drink caffeine all day and stare into our bright screens all night. We make to-do lists in our minds and then watch the plodding minutes on the clock while stressing about how tired we will be in the morning. Finally, when we can't get rest, we turn to alcohol or drugs to knock us out, which come with their own side effects and don't actually give you quality sleep.

Because I had a hard time falling asleep, I started to think that sleep was an inefficient use of my time, and I started working more in the night. But experts argue that you're not being more productive. "You could stay up and putter away at a repetitive tedious task, but if you want to do something where you have to think clearly and be effective in your work, you're far better off getting sleep," Brian James Murray, associate professor of neurology and director of the sleep laboratory at Toronto's Sunnybrook Health Sciences Centre, told me. "Studies have shown that if you stay up a lot, you can still continue doing a menial, simple task, but you'll make more errors, and you'll be less aware that you're making errors."

So, prioritize your sleep. Develop good sleep hygiene. At bedtime, be like a Mogwai/Gremlin — avoid bright lights (from screens) and don't eat anything at night.

Some more tips to get better sleep:

- Keep the room completely dark and quiet.
- If you're not asleep in 30 minutes, get out of bed and return only when you're sleepy. You should associate your bed only with sleep and sexy time. And lying around will only stress you out. You're

better off getting out and doing something relaxing like reading for a short while.

- Remove your clock from your view. Looking at it makes your insomnia worse.
- Lower the temperature.
- Expose yourself to sunlight during the day and simulate dusk by dimming the lights for the hours before bed.
- Institute a bedtime routine with quiet activity such as reading or meditation and ban screen time an hour ahead.
- Limit your caffeine later in the day. If you drink coffee in the morning, a quarter of the caffeine is still in your system at 10 p.m.

And if you want to discuss the finer points of various frog-in-the-rain soundtracks, you know where to find me.

The double-F approach and other secrets to a happy diet

I'm clearly not a nutritionist, given that, on some busy mornings, I'll eat year-old Halloween candy for breakfast. But we don't need to be health nuts to know that what we eat affects our mood. Research shows that diet can influence brain chemistry. A 2017 Australian study showed that over a 12-week period, 30% of its patients saw improvements in their feelings of depression after adopting a healthier diet.

To keep your mood up, nutritionists suggest that you keep hydrated; avoid processed food, excess sugar and white refined carbs; eat good fats and regular meals to keep your blood sugar steady and ward off the hanger.

Holistic nutritionist Kim D'Eon says balancing your blood sugar is the place to start when you're looking to improve your mood: "Glucose feeds the brain, so you want it to be nice and steady, not a roller-coaster ride of ups and downs."

We should also be feeding our gut's microbiome (home to your body's bacteria) to be happier. "Our gut is the primary place of manufacture for our 'happy hormone' serotonin," D'Eon explains. "To nurture that ecosystem of microbes, start with a double-F approach."

This sounds like I'm supposed to hold up two middle fingers at some food, but she means to get more fibre and ferments into our diets. Fibre like plant foods (fruits, vegetables, nuts, seeds and legumes) and fermented food (sauerkraut, kimchi, kombucha and kefir, which are loaded with probiotics).

You tend to eat healthier when you meal-plan, bring your own lunch to work or make your own family dinner, versus buying restaurant fare. You also save money.

Of course, eating healthier can be more expensive than eating junk food. My thrifty mother-in-law can buy five frozen meals from a discount store called Almost Perfect for the price of a kale salad kit. (Seriously, this very humble store exists. As does the Bleu Marine restaurant in Beijing with this tagline: "Probably the best steak in town." Probably. Maybe. Next door's steak might be better.)

Your health, like your money, is an investment and worthy of your effort and long-term planning. Here are a few ways we can integrate happy, healthier and affordable eating in our lives.

- Mindful meal Mondays. For one meal, even if it's a five-minute coffee break, put down your phone and just eat. Taste your food. Chew your food. Pay attention to the texture. The sounds. Breathe. This will also help you be more attuned to feelings of fullness and aid with digestion.

- In an effort to spend more quality time together, a married couple I know joined a weekly cooking class. The food they made in class gave them leftovers for days.
- My friends get together every Sunday, split the cost of groceries, cook and prepare meals for the rest of the week. Consider organizing a soup or stew or pasta swap; this rescues you from eating your cauldron of jambalaya over the next month.
- Save the treats for the weekend. Mofo and I try to eat healthy and homemade in the week and then treat ourselves come Friday night. To fight cravings, we have oatmeal energy balls in the fridge, trail mix or fruit in the car and other healthy snacks on hand. We falter (Halloween and Christmas are killer), but we keep trying.
- When possible, eat foods that are in season. It's healthier, cheaper and better for the planet. Win, win, win.
- Freeze extra portions of healthy meals in single-serving containers for when plans fall through or you need lunch in a jiffy.

I know that preaching more sleep, exercise and healthy eating is the most obvious advice in the universe. I know that they seem like big mountains to climb. But like saving for retirement or getting out of debt, they are mountains you can conquer. You just have to start and go with the momentum. Changing one habit can create a chain reaction, positively affecting your other habits. *New York Times* reporter Charles Duhigg calls them keystone habits. Someone who commits to eating more healthily, for example, will be empowered by that victory; suddenly, because you're someone who takes care of yourself, you're also the type of person who will be more responsible with money.

We chase and spend money in the pursuit of happiness. But if we're exhausted, energy broke and our blood sugar is plummeting, that pursuit will be even more futile. Health is wealth.

YOUR HAPPY MONEY TO-DO LIST

- I know. If you had time for exercise, you'd be doing it already. Pencil in a 30-minute walk on your lunch break with a work colleague; take the stairs to her cubicle. Email your friends, co-workers or OHM tribe right now to ask who will be your workout buddy and who promises to guilt you if you skip boxing class.
- Make sleep a priority. And good quality sleep — free from booze or pills.
- Eat your next meal slowly, without distractions. Put your fork down between bites. Stop when you are full. Think about everything that went into this meal: who cooked it, who planted and harvested the ingredients, who supported them, what went into its creation (water, soil), etc. #gratitude
- Commit to yourself, to your OHM tribe or to your person that you're going to try to break or create a habit. Pick something very achievable that you can do on a daily basis (take the stairs

at the office, order a medium instead of your normal large, drink an extra glass of water a day, turn the lights down an hour before bedtime, etc.). If you mess up, start again and maybe make the habit even easier. You're not failing, so don't mourn. Health is a lifestyle and an ongoing journey — just keep going.

- Do a weekly challenge with someone. Every day, Mofo and I give each other a point for at least five happy tasks (gratitude, stretching, exercise, early bedtime, etc.). We post our progress on the fridge, and we compete to see who will emerge with the most points by the end of the week.

MONEY TALKS

- Would you rather be tired from lack of sleep but enjoy fun activities and work opportunities or miss out on things and be well rested? Would you rather have two extra hours of sleep or one extra day added to the weekend?
- When and why do you tend to eat poorly or binge-eat?
- When was the last time that you exercised and forgot you were exercising? Is there a way of getting more of that in your life?

TAKE STOCK, MAKE GAINS

*Let's figure out where you are and where
you need to be. Get pumped.*

13
BALANCE THE BILLS AND THRILLS

I get it. The "B" word.

Budgeting is limiting. Budgeting is awareness of the sins of our wallet. Budgeting is delayed gratification. Budgeting is tedious nerd work. And none of that makes you happy. (Unless you're a money nerd and budgeting is ecstasy.)

A budget looks like restriction, but it can provide freedom. Freedom for you to be true to your values. Freedom for you to spend without guilt. Freedom from debating every little purchase. With a budget, your money will have a purpose. You will be living, saving and spending with intention.

Listen, I am not saying you should budget every day of your life. I don't think that you should track every pack of mints you buy until your teeth fall out. But if money just disappears as if some reverse tooth fairy is raiding your wallet, you should know where it's going. And if you've had a period where you've lost your way and overspent, maybe over the summer or the holidays, a budget can help you press the reset button.

When I say that you need to create a budget, all I mean is that you need to create a strategy for your money. Call it a budget, a spending plan, a cash flow statement, whatever you want. It's your blueprint for happy money. Let's set up the blueprint and get on with our lives, okay?

First take stock

Like many of my firsts — my first kiss, my first time driving a stick shift — creating my first budget was a cringeworthy and anxiety-inducing experience. When I started my first adult job, every week, almost $800 was added to my bank account. In my first year of work, I spent almost all of that money. On rent. On travel. And on miscellaneous stuff. What miscellaneous stuff? I have no idea. I'd never budgeted before (unless you count Halloween candy). I wanted to treat myself for working hard. I filled my home and my life with stuff that I thought a fabulous adult with a salary should have. I bought an $800 entertainment system with a subwoofer (which I was assured was important but sounds like a nickname you give to a hotdog). I bought a $150 MP3 player to replace my Discman that when clipped to my butt, bounced like a spaceship repeatedly crash-landing on the moon. I bought a suit jacket and pencil skirt (that I never wore) because I might have to attend a meeting and look uber professional. I remember feeling guilty about not saving money, but I was aimless when it came to financial goals.

A friend of mine who was a financial advisor gave me my first budget spreadsheet so I could see where my money was going. I put off filling it out because I just didn't want to know about my money. (It was like how I don't want to know what's in my soft-serve ice cream. I won't be able to pronounce most of the ingredients and knowing will ruin the goodness.)

When I finally went through my bank statements for the previous month, I was shocked at the amount of money I had spent eating out: I was probably spending more than $1,000 a month on dining. For one. I was working 10 to 12 hours a day and I never cooked. (I rectified this in later years when I took a culinary arts course with my best friend — money well spent.)

The figure in my shopping category also seemed bloated. I had learned my mom's impulse to buy things on sale. I bought random stuff and justified the purchases by saying they were on sale. Oh God. Warehouse sales. Liquidation outlets. Boxing Day door crashers. To this day, when I open a drawer in my dining room, I have to push aside two boxes of napkins I bought on sale. They are pink and turquoise and shaped like a pregnant lady. I bought them at least 10 years ago to use when one of my friends got pregnant. (No one would be pregnant for years, and even when the day came, the napkins never made it out.) I should get rid of them. Sunk cost, right?

The exercise of creating a budget blew my mind. It motivated me to make adjustments. If you've never created a budget for your everyday expenses, do it. If you're married, consider doing one for the family. We all want to feel in control and that our money is being well spent — a budget kick-starts that.

The art of the sexy budget

Okay, I'm going to make budgeting sexy to keep you enthused. My sister-in-law writes popular steamy romance novels, so let me use her work as inspiration. (I'm really trying to give you your money's worth for this book.)

50 Shades of Green:
How to do a budget in three hot moves

1. Find some time. Set the mood. Put the phone on silent. Pour a glass of wine. Turn on some tunes.
2. With hungry eyes, scan your bulging bills, your lean pay stubs, your turgid bank statements . . .
3. If you prefer the flick of cash versus the tap of plastic, mm-hmm, that's good. But for one month, grab every single one of your receipts and slide them in between the folds . . . of your wallet or stuff them in your fanny . . . pack.

Okay. Okay. Fine. I promise to never write erotica again. (And I didn't even get into our money moving in and out.)

Throwing pornographic personal finance out the window, here are four real steps to creating your budget.

1. Gather the numbers to populate your awesome budget — everything that you've spent money on in the previous month — and categorize them. Your cellphone bill. Your lunches out. Your gym membership. This is your retrospective budget. Write it out by hand, use an app or plug the numbers into a downloadable spreadsheet.

2. If you have annual expenses or one-time costs such as memberships, divide those by 12 for your monthly plan.

3. For motivation, tell your OHM tribe or promise someone that you're going to finish your retrospective budget by the end of the week.

4. If that goes well, try going back two more months. Three months is a good snapshot of your regular money habits. If you're self-employed and income fluctuates from month to month, you might be better off doing a budget with annual numbers. You can still do your monthly expenses, just multiply them by 12.

Once you have tallied all of the numbers and filled in the categories, the most important thing to look for? That you earn more than you spend. This is the first key to money success. If your income is higher than your expenses, high-five, fist bump, platonic hug and kiss. If I could fly a plane, my aerial banner would read, "Earn more than you spend."

Now with your income and all of your expenses laid out before you, you'll see what you need to live (essential expenses) and you'll see how you spend to enjoy life (discretionary expenses).

Essential expenses include housing (rent, mortgage, condo fees), utilities, food, transportation, medical expenses, child care, insurance and taxes.

Discretionary expenses (or fun money) include entertainment, dining, clothing, personal care, gifts, vacations, electronics, cable/Netflix, robot vacuums and heated toilet seats. (I also include a category called miscellaneous for the random things that might come up.)

I put my savings in the essential category, along with paying back debt. This might not be doable right away; if it isn't, scan your discretionary expenses for cost savings and make a goal of putting something, anything in savings. I need my savings for future me to live and be happy. I'm the boss. And I pay the boss first. (Saving 10% to 20% of your after-tax income is a good start, but more on that later.)

Once you've completed your budget, take a moment. Maybe you're super pumped up and ready to make changes, like your first day at the gym. Maybe you're sweating, feeling hopeless, ashamed and worried about the work ahead, like your first day at the gym. Whatever you feel, it's okay. As your (financial) fitness buddy, I'm already proud. Doing a budget is no small feat. Let's keep going.

TECH SUPPORT

Of course, technology can help with all of this.

One of the most popular free money apps out there is Mint. With more than 16 million users around the world, Mint pulls all of your financial information from the bank accounts that you add into one dashboard.

It's smart and intuitive. It breaks your expenses automatically into different categories. (Who doesn't love a pie chart? It reminds you of dessert!) You can set budget limits, and you get alerts when you go over that budget. It also tells you when bills are due. I used Mint for a few years, but I cancelled my profile when I got a good handle on my behaviour and the benefits stopped outweighing the risks. The risks? Well, you share all of your banking IDs and passwords with this financial aggregator. If something were to ever happen — like a hacker breaking into your account and stealing your money — you sharing your passwords with Mint might put you in breach of your cardholder agreement and void your security guarantee with your bank. Your bank promises to return any money that was stolen from you due to fraud, but you have to agree to its conditions — one of which is not sharing your password with anyone (including your spouse). But still, millions love this app.

There are other apps that don't require your passwords, such as You Need a Budget (YNAB) and Wally. With these programs, you have to input all of the data yourself. Wally is free; it allows you to take pictures of receipts, and it will populate your budget with the information; it also uses GPS to see where you're spending your money. People have said that programs like YNAB and Wally create more mindfulness around spending because you're thinking about your spending every time you log a purchase.

How you too can have guilt-free spendapaloozas

This is how you can have your cake and save it too. We've looked at the numbers, and we now know how much you need to live (how to keep the lights on at your house, etc.).

We also have an idea of what we spend to enjoy living ($11 a month to binge-watch *Friends* on Netflix).

Now physically separate these pools of money. Create separate bank accounts for them.

The best thing that came out of my budget was that I created a spending account. After all of my survival needs were met (remember to include savings), I determined an amount that I would like to spend on fun every month. I opened up a no-fee bank account with a debit card. Every week, I siphoned money from my chequing account into this spending account, and it gave me a guilt-free way to spend. (If you have bigger short-term goals, like a wedding or a vacation, you might open up a separate savings account for that. Money maven Gail Vaz-Oxlade wouldn't call that savings but "planned spending," which is a great way to frame it.)

The first few times I realized that I was free to spend, let me tell you, I felt glorious. Like realizing that you're home alone and you don't have to wear pants.

My chequing account was for essential expenses (mortgage payments, insurance, retirement savings, emergency savings, debt repayment, groceries, etc.). I also kept some regular automated payments coming out of this account, such as my cellphone bill, to avoid any chance that a payment would bounce and affect my credit score. And I tried not to use the debit card associated with my chequing account. Eventually, I left it at home and only carried the debit card linked to my spending account.

The spending account was for my enjoyment. Whatever I wanted. As long as there was money in the spending account, I could buy dinner for friends. I could pick up that pair of shoes. I could go to that concert. If I used my credit card, it was paid for from my spending account. If I knew

I had a big purchase coming up, I'd try to cut back in the weeks prior to bulk up the account.

I can't tell you a percentage or dollar figure for how much you should spend on fun every month; some like more, some are good with less. But I had taken the stress out of spending because I knew I had taken care of my priorities. I didn't have to feel guilty about buying.

Let's say after you've covered your essential expenses, put aside some money for savings and for fighting debt, you end up with very little. If you think, "This is bull. I can't enjoy life with this paltry sum," keep reading.

Going with the flow

To simplify your life and create more room for joy, automate as many transfers, withdrawals and bill payments as possible. Just make sure that you're looking at your bank statements to double-check the numbers.

Here are the basics of managing the flow of your cash.

1. Your employer pays you. They might deduct money for a group retirement fund (and hopefully matches some or all of it), in addition to making government deductions.
2. Your income ends up in your chequing account. From here, you pay your bills: rent, mortgage, utilities. From this account, set up automatic transfers to your savings accounts and for debt repayment.
3. Set up an automatic transfer from your chequing account to your spending account. This is your happy money fund. Buy whatever makes you happy.

4. From your spending account, pay off your credit card and withdraw cash to spend.

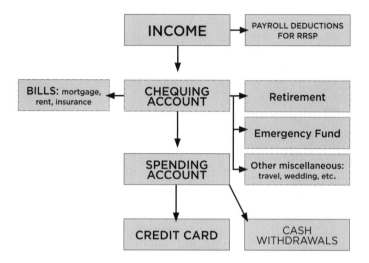

With your spending and savings accounts and your automated transfers, your money blueprint is like a self-driving car. Sit back, enjoy the ride — but keep an eye on the road to make sure you're moving in the right direction.

Budgeting for what matters

We all have limited financial resources, and since we can't buy everything, we have to prioritize. That's Adulting 101. Before you buy, I suggested that you ask yourself a question: "Is the way that I am spending my money in line with my values?"

What are the top five things that you value most in life? Here are mine.

1. Relationships
2. Well-being

3. Creativity
4. Kindness
5. Adventure

Now try this exercise. Look at your discretionary expenses — what you spend on to enjoy your life. In the last month, what are the top five things you spent money on? For example:

1. Clothing, $350
2. Restaurants, $200
3. Photography seminar, $100
4. Grooming/beauty, $75
5. Cellphone plan, $60

Do your top five lists overlap in any way? Using the above example, the only true overlap is "photography seminar" and "creativity." You could argue that you need your cellphone plan to maintain relationships. Or that you need to wax your back hair to keep your girlfriend. But as I've said before, check yourself when it comes to justifying your spending.

If there's no overlap, how can you devote more of your resources to your top values? Where can you spend less to be spending in a more fulfilling way?

Remember you're in control. You're the Bachelorette/Bachelor and your budget is like your rose ceremony. You're the star and everything is available for your happiness; all you have to do is dole out the flowers to the choices that truly fulfill you.

Looking for waste and extra dollars

Things that annoy me:

- A toilet paper roll with one remaining square
- When menstruating women say "their friend" is visiting; what kind of horrible friends do you have?!?
- Money wasted (unused automatic subscriptions, insufficient funds charges, etc.)

The awesome thing about your budget is that you now have a snapshot of what could be dragging you down. Where are you wasting your dollars? Where can you find more money to go to the things that you really value?

Spend some time going through each line of your budget and ask, "Could I spend less money here?" "Do I need to have this or do this? Do I even use this?" "Is there a cheaper alternative that would still be fine?" "How happy did this make me at the time?" "How happy does it make me now?"

Look through your bank statements and make sure that you don't have any so-called zombie charges on it — bills that haunt you even though you've killed your service or membership. Watch out for free-trial memberships that you sign up for and forget about so you're being charged because you didn't cancel. Identify the other kind of zombie spending — the mindless spending that you do on autopilot, stuff that you buy as a habit but doesn't make you happy.

On the flip side, when it comes to your resources, how can you squeeze a little more from that fruit? For example, does your employer offer coverage for massage therapy that you could use for a spa day? Do you have unused gift cards languishing in your wallet that you could sell on a resale site like Raise.com or CardSwap.ca? Are you ignoring your rewards points?

There's a subculture of savvy people who are pros at collecting and maximizing their rewards points — from getting signing bonuses to shopping at stores where you get extra points (including online shopping portals run by the credit cards). I'm not saying spend more to get more, and beware that if you're paying interest, those points are *not* a good deal. But if you're not carrying a balance, could you make the most of what you have? For example, if what you live for is dinner and movies, eat at restaurants where you can earn and redeem points for free movies.

Remember anything that you cut needs to be reallocated to your goals. Otherwise you're wringing precious water from a towel only to pour it into another towel — or down the drain.

HOW TO SAVE MONEY ON THREE THINGS YOU THOUGHT YOU COULDN'T SAVE MONEY ON

With some bills, we tend to set them and forget them. But even your fixed costs deserve another look. Here are three examples of where a few phone calls and some work around the house can get you more money to devote to other things that will make you happier.

Call your car and home insurance company and see if you can get a better deal. If you bundle your car and home insurance with the same company, you'll get an average of 15% in savings. You and your spouse will get further savings if you both use the same insurer. Has there been a change in your circumstances that means you'll be driving less? Did you get a new job closer to home? Are you going on maternity leave for a year? When I let my auto insurance company know that I would no longer be commuting to work every day, my premiums dropped by $150 a year. Also, pay in a lump sum. If you pay your premiums monthly, you might be facing some extra administrative fees. If the one-time fee is too much to stomach, set money aside every month to cover the premium when it comes time to renew.

If you're unhappy with your telecom plan, call and ask to be transferred to the customer retention department. Also, shop around and be armed with information. If you don't watch the golf channel, downgrade your cable plan. If you don't enjoy cable, dump it. If you don't need a landline, cut it. If you don't need the latest and greatest digital toy, consider buying your own phone and getting a cheaper plan; some service providers have a bring-your-own-device discount. Are you paying for extra things when you don't use them? I cancelled my $4 value pack with my cellphone provider because I didn't need 35 voicemail spots for my mom to leave me 35 messages.

To lower your utility bills, install a programmable thermostat. Do your laundry outside of peak hours. Cut energy vampires: switch off your computer when you're not using it ($16 in savings a year), unplug chargers ($3), turn off a single light ($4). Install a high-efficiency showerhead (save $22 a year in electricity). Stop drafts with weather stripping ($8). Switch to compact fluorescent light bulbs and save $5 a year per bulb. Good for you. Good for the environment. Happiness for all.

Bring on the FOMOOOO
(fear of missing out on other opportunities)

When we look at our limited funds, we understand that there are trade-offs. But what we don't often appreciate is the full weight of our trade-offs in the long term. For example, if you're going to put a $500 item on your credit card and take a year to pay it off, then the item isn't $500. After interest, you'll have spent closer to $600, plus the added stress of carrying the balance.

The other thing to consider is the opportunity cost.

I interviewed a 30-year-old human resources worker who went out for drinks with her colleagues every Thursday. Every time, she spent about $40 (maybe $55 if she had appetizers or food and maybe $60 if she took a taxi home). At a minimum, that's $2,080 a year. That might be a perfectly acceptable price to pay for connecting with colleagues and bosses, for networking opportunities, for a mental reprieve from a hard week. But would you pay more than $200,000 for it? If she invested $2,080 every year in her tax-free savings account until she was 65, with an average rate of return of 5%, she'd have that chunk saved for retirement.

Every item in your budget is a trade-off. But at least when everything is laid out before you, you're better able to make informed decisions that you and future you will be happy with.

YOUR HAPPY MONEY TO-DO LIST

- Tell someone, anyone, that you're going to create a retrospective budget and look back over three months of spending.
- Create a happy money blueprint that will give you spending goals going forward.
- Download your bank's app on your phone for easier access to your balance and to keep track of your purchases. Check it once a week to make sure there are no errors such as double charges.
- Open a no-fee or low-fee chequing account with an associated debit card. This is your spending account. Create an automatic transfer of money into this account every one or two weeks.
- Go looking for extra happy money. Take a peek at your monthly bills and bank and credit card statements. Trim something, then add that amount, even if it's only $20, to your savings plan or to your happy spending plan so you don't spend it elsewhere.

MONEY TALKS

- Name a category that you should put more of your money in. Is there some other category where that could come from, given your spending plan?
- If you've had a budget in the past, what about it worked for you? What didn't you like?

14
CHECK YOUR WORTH

You're well on your journey to your happy money place. Now is a good time to pause and pinpoint where you are. What do you have going for you? What are your assets, aside from your good looks? Sabrina Geremia at Google Canada encourages everyone to "be the CEO of your own life, your career, your choices and family." A good boss knows the value of the business she is building. First, let's look at some numbers, boss.

Your outer net worth

To track my family's financial progress, I calculate our net worth twice a year. And I like to see this number climb every time. Your net worth is the value of all of your assets minus your liabilities. Basically, what you own after subtracting what you owe.

This isn't a city-wide contest. We don't display our net worth on our shirts. No one needs to know it but you (and maybe your financial advisor and your mom because you're proud). Your number today is the benchmark against which you'll measure your success.

You can use an online calculator like the one at BankRate.com; your bank may also have a net worth calculator on its website. You can also input numbers into a spreadsheet. When I was single, I used paper and a pen. Old school. Now, I share a Google spreadsheet with my husband so we can update and track it together. I assure you that when it comes to money, ignorance is not bliss. This snapshot will help you draw a map to a better place.

To calculate your net worth, first list your assets and their current value, including

- Cash (chequing account, savings account)
- Investments (mutual funds, stocks, bonds, ETFs, retirement plans, life insurance cash value)
- Personal assets (vehicles you own, collectibles, pinball machines)
- Property (primary home, vacation home, rental property)

Then list your current liabilities — that's money you owe — and their balances:

- Line of credit, credit card, car lease, mortgages, unpaid taxes, student loans, taxes due and so on.

Once you know where you are, you can turn your attentions to where you want to go. Maybe your net worth is a negative, but that doesn't mean it will always stay there. Your net worth will rise as you pay down your debt, as you build equity in your home, as your investments grow. It could change if your house price drops, or if the dog chews up your complete first-edition Pokémon card set that's potentially worth thousands.

If your net worth is rising from year to year, you are living within your means. You are earning and saving more than you spend. And you are on track to retire happily. High-five.

COMMONLY ASKED QUESTIONS (AND ANSWERS) WHEN CALCULATING YOUR NET WORTH

I think my home makes me a bagillionaire. How do I find out the current value of my house?

Yes, your home is probably your biggest asset. Research how much similar homes in your area have sold for or ask a real estate agent for an estimate. To get super accurate, deduct the real estate commission and lawyer fees you'd pay in selling the home. Some financial advisors will dissuade people from including their principal residence when calculating their net worth for fear that people will rely too much on their home as their retirement nest egg. The key to the net worth is not so much getting the perfect number; the key is making sure you track and update the number the same way every time. Include your home or don't include it.

Just understand that money in your home is the hardest to access if you need to live off that cash. And understand that if the housing market has an upswing or a dive, this greatly affects your number.

How do I figure out the current value of my depreciating asset — I mean, my car?

Use Autotrader or online quotes to get an estimate of what your car is worth, if you own it and were to sell it today.

Despite what my boyfriend says, my Star Wars collectibles are assets. Can I include those in my net worth?

Sure, if you're willing to part with them (or let your boyfriend sell them). Look for online price guide books or ask a collector what your toys will sell for. Remember your art or collectibles are only worth what someone will pay.

The last time I checked, I'm not dead yet. So, does my life insurance count as part of my net worth?

It depends. Some life insurance policies — whole life and universal life, for example — count as assets because they have a cash value. (The cash value is what the insurance company will pay you if you cancel a policy early.) To determine the cash-surrender value, contact your insurance agent or look at your policy statement. If this last bit about insurance made you super excited, I devote an entire section to life insurance later. Whoopee for you.

I have a unicorn: a magical pension from work. Is that part of my net worth?
If you quit work today, you could receive a lump sum from your pension plan. This money is called "the commuted value" and could be included in your net worth. You'll have to ask HR for that figure. I have no advice on how to do this without alarming anyone in your company.

My aunt Linda has promised to give me all of her money when she dies. She's pretty damn healthy, but she's just getting into base jumping so . . .
Do not include your potential inheritance. That is a hypothetical asset. Yes, you might be the favourite child today but that's before you married you-know-who; plus your brother's been upping his lawn mowing and show shovelling game.

Your inner net worth

My inner net worth is always fluctuating. When I was younger, my self-esteem was subterranean. I was constantly trying to prove my worth — to my father, my grandfather, my peers and my toughest critic, myself. When I was 18, I got a small tattoo of the Chinese character for "love" on my back as a resolution to love myself more. I should have put it somewhere more visible because many a time, I've forgotten that I got it, spotted it in the mirror and freaked out, thinking that a spider was creeping into my pants.

Over the years, I've looked for ways to feel more confident; there are sloughs of scientific studies on things to do, like listening to bass-heavy music, dressing for success and channeling a celebrity (love yourself the way Kanye loves Kanye). But what follows is how I fuel my worth.

- Surround yourself with uplifting, supportive people. Some friends bring you down: you feel drained after hanging with them, they're resentful of your success or have a value system that you don't agree with. Maybe they're super judgey and when you're together, you gossip and judge others (judging others trains your brain to also harshly judge yourself). If I ever feel low, I just need to think about how my best friend, Kerry, talks about me. Seriously, I wish I could shrink her, stick her in my pocket and pull her out to announce my arrival everywhere.
- Pay attention to the way that you talk about yourself. Is your inner critic more Simon Cowell than Ellen DeGeneres? Catch yourself and tell Simon to STFU. World-renowned psychology researcher Barbara Fredrickson determined that a ratio of three positive thoughts to one negative thought is what determines if you flourish; so, for every negative thing that you think you've done, think of three good things you've accomplished. At my local chapter of Girls Inc., a not-for-profit group that empowers girls, when

one of the girls says something negative about herself, the other girls shout, "Give me three!" and she has to immediately come up with three positive things. (An example from my life: "I made up the word 'imaginatary' on live TV. But I appeared relaxed. I used a lot of actual words. I made the hosts laugh.")

- Recognize perfectionism as an enemy to confidence. Do you have trouble meeting your own standards or have you ever been told that your standards, are too high? Let go. It's okay to fail. It's okay to apply for a job even if you don't meet 100% of the criteria. It's okay to learn as you go. It's okay to take action even if you don't feel totally ready. It's okay to look stupid at something so long as you took a risk. Everyone who matters will love you the same.

- Gain confidence by doing. Give it a whirl. If I don't understand something, I try to learn about it. If I feel as if I'm not good at something, I work more and harder. If I'm unsure, I get feedback and I reflect. If I'm insecure in one area, I build up another area that I value.

- When your self-confidence is waning, what would someone who loves you say? I think about what I would say to my own son. "Work. Work so that you can look at yourself in the mirror and feel like you've put in the effort to meet your own standards. But never, ever think that you have to build your self-worth. You are worthy. You were worthy the day that you were born. Work to recognize that your worth already exists."

To assess and highlight your inner worth, here are three exercises where you can do the work too.

1. How am I rich? (Do not put anything in here that is monetary or material.)

"I am rich in ___."

"I am rich in ___."

"I am rich in ___."

Answer this question at least once a month. Share it with your best friend or partner or OHM tribe and ask for theirs.

2. How am I growing?

"In recent years, I've learned _____ [a lesson, a skill, a strength] and I've been able to improve life or give back through _____."

3. What do others value about me?

Ask a friend or loved one or mentor or trusted co-worker for your top three qualities and specific examples of these strengths.

Possible email request: "Tell me how awesome I am!" or: "Hey, I'm doing a self-assessment exercise, and I'd like to ask for your feedback to help me identify my strengths. What do you consider to be my top three qualities and an example of each? Thanks in advance for the ego boost, and let me know if you need one too."

Possible email request if you'd like to just pay it forward:

> This is a chain letter with the sole purpose of spreading joy. All you have to do is choose someone in your life and answer two questions. Then email/text/post this to spread the joy. I chose _____.

1. Name one of your favourite qualities about this person.
2. Describe a time that reflects this.

For every person that you forward this to, Microsoft will not pay you any money. If you don't forward this, your sex life will not be cursed by Bloody Mary for seven years. But if you choose to forward this, may it bring you (and others) joy.

This might seem hokey — I assure you that I haven't suddenly morphed into a Care Bear — but it will help keep things in perspective. Your outer/numerical net worth is not a measure of your happiness. It should not be correlated with your self-worth. Nothing that you buy and no amount of money will make you more or less worthy. Remember you were worthy the day that you were born.

YOUR HAPPY MONEY TO-DO LIST

- Calculate your net worth: what you own minus what you owe. Use this magic number as a benchmark for your success.
- Identify your top three best qualities and list examples of how they've come into play in the last week. Resolve to learn something new this week or practice something that you feel insecure about.
- Agree that from now on, you and your OHM tribe are going to help boost each other's self-worth. Pick one person from the tribe and practise out loud how you're going to introduce them (and others) from now on. "This is my friend

Uresha. She counsels at-risk youth and has just launched her own successful business." We have to hold each other up to the light.

- Send an email or text to three friends or mentors or family members. Ask them what your top three strengths are and examples of them. At the next outing with your best friend or at bedtime with your spouse, take turns telling each other what you think their best qualities are. Yep. It's a love fest.

MONEY TALKS

- What do you have in your life (not money or stuff) that makes you rich?
- What is most important to you in life right now? What must you have in life in order to feel fulfilled?
- How do you measure your goodness?

15
GOAL DIGGER

Several years ago, I wrote two teen vampire novels. I know. What do vampires have to do with money? Well, they live forever — and that means a lot of savings are required. I self-published the books as a passion project, and they ended up selling more than 70,000 copies around the world. People often ask how I completed those projects while working full-time and dancing part-time.

First, I got nerdy. I created a goals chart, dividing the year into quarters with specific weekly goals. I checked in with a writing buddy every Sunday and reported my progress. (My goal was to write 2,500 words a week to complete a 60,000-word book in six months.)

A study at Dominican University in California confirmed that 76% of individuals had accomplished their goals or were at least halfway there after writing down their goals, sharing them with a friend and then sending regular progress reports.

I always make sure I have SMART goals (who doesn't love mnemonic acronyms): specific, measurable, attainable, realistic and time-bound. A goal of, say, "Getting a J-Lo bottom" isn't as actionable as "doing 100 squats every day for six months." The same goes for money goals. A goal of "saving my effing money" sounds motivating because of the profanity, but "save $50 every month for a year so I can afford to be in my bestie's bridal party" will gear you up for success. Now that you've sorted out your budget and know what to aim for, let's talk about how to get after it.

Your kill list

What do you want to accomplish? Write out a list of five things that you'd like to achieve (which involve money). Anything. It might be getting the credit card balance to zero. Asking for a raise. Understanding what the heck is going on in your retirement accounts.

Pick one of your goals and break it down into tiny, bite-sized goals; give yourself a specific task immediately.

For example, let's take on the debt.

> **Goal:** Pay off the credit card. The balance? $10,000. 18% interest rate.
> **Plan:** Get this sucker to zero by committing $600 a month.
> **Timeline:** One year, eight months.

So where does that $600 a month come from?

Well, let's say the lease for my Honda Civic is up next month, and I've decided that I'll find alternative transit until the debt is cleared. That's $480 freed up (monthly lease payment and insurance). I pay about $150 in gas a month but that will now go to my transit pass. I still need to find an extra $120 a month. That's $30 a week. I often spend that and more on lunches out with co-workers. I'll commit to bringing my lunch four days a week — with a treat on Friyay.

Often, I hear people say, "I'm not giving up my car, my room, my shopping . . ." But sometimes, it takes a short-term setback to win the game. I have friends who rent out their condos on Airbnb for a week or weekend and crash at another friend's house or stay with their parents. Other friends of mine used to rent a room in their house to international students. I know a couple who went from two cars to one to save money for fertility treatments.

We think sacrifice will make us unhappy. But maybe it won't. Maybe it'll give you more power because you just might feel pride for taking some control. Doing something hard can still be rewarding. Consider it like running a financial marathon: it probably won't be easy, but you'll be euphoric when you cross the finish line.

Everything in moderation versus all or nothing

We used to call my husband and our best friend "Sugar Shane and Diabetes Don" (names have been changed to protect their dignities). They were black holes for desserts. If cut, they'd bleed honey.

But in the last year, both have attacked their vices in their own ways. Diabetes Don is what author Gretchen Rubin calls an abstainer. He initiated a strict processed-sugar strike. Zero processed sugar. Not even a single grain. Sugar Shane, on the other hand, is what Rubin would call a moderator. He decided that from Monday to Thursday, he eats healthily, but on the weekend, he can splurge.

Are you an abstainer or a moderator? If you tell yourself that you cannot spend on *anything* fun until you pay off your credit card bill, will you get pissed and go on a cathartic but destructive shoe binge? (Me.) Or is it easier if you say "no" to everything fun for now because then there's no inner conflict for you? (Diabetes Don.)

Remember your goals have to be realistic. Ambition is fantastic, but it didn't matter how many times I chanted, "I must, I must, I must increase my bust" while doing chest exercises as a teenager — it didn't work, and I gave up.

Do what works for you. And don't beat yourself up if you break your own rules. Just try again. In life, that's what counts.

Personally, I think Diabetes Don is a masochist. But to be supportive, when he comes over, I bake him a separate dessert with dates or bananas as sweeteners. Still tasty, he says.

Small, achievable wins

Giant goals can be demotivating. For example, paying down your mortgage could feel impossible if you can't see your progress. Studies show that people prefer to pay down the debts with the lowest balance, rather than the ones with the highest interest rate, because it makes them feel good to cross that debt out.

I get that. I love making mundane checklists. I have successfully completed many tasks today — do laundry, pay bills, buy bread — and that spurs me on to do more. Our brains like the small, frequent rewards over the exceptional big ones.

You'll also be more motivated if your brain thinks you're closer to success. Happiness researcher Shawn Achor refers to a marathoner's "X-spot," where runners can see the finish line and their brains release chemicals and they can speed up. If you make a checklist, make yourself feel a little closer to the finish line by including a few things you've already accomplished. If you're starting to save $100 a month for your wedding, start by depositing $250 of birthday money in an account.

And if you get frustrated, try not to moan about how much further you have to go. Take a moment and look at how far you've come. Look at the things you've already checked off and the steps you've already taken.

Celebrate those wins. I wouldn't recommend celebrating a savings goal by spending the equivalent amount on a gift for yourself. But have a reward for your milestones. A dessert with dates or bananas, maybe.

Buddy up

They call it the love hormone. When we hug or kiss a loved one, when we have sex or breastfeed, oxytocin levels rise. Maybe we should also call it the generosity hormone or the secret money weapon. Paul Zak, one of the pioneers of neuroeconomics, says oxytocin increases charitable giving and helps us delay gratification. In his research, he found that the more researchers introduced oxytocin in test subjects through nasal inhalers, the more generous they were with money.

Oxytocin also increases people's patience. Test subjects were given either oxytocin or placebos and asked to choose options to earn money. You could get money now or wait several weeks and get more later. Those who had been infused with oxytocin were more willing to delay the immediate gratification for a larger reward; the chemical increased patience by 43%, Zak says.

When faced with saving decisions, wouldn't it be great to have inhalers at the ready to squirt oxytocin up our noses?

Since they aren't available, to naturally increase our oxytocin levels, connect with your OHM tribe or with other loved ones. If you meet to discuss your goals, start the day with hugs (natural oxytocin producers).

Another way for your squad to help you take care of business is to make your savings goals public. Make it a family affair. I've heard of one family putting a paper snake on the wall for everyone to see and the kids would snip away at it every time the family paid off a chunk of debt. Buddy up with someone to check in on your progress. Even if you are not comfortable being specific about your goals, just talk about whether you've achieved said secret goals. In a study of Chilean entrepreneurs, those who reported weekly to a peer group deposited 3.5 times more often into their savings account, and their average balance was almost twice of those not receiving peer support.

Cue cards

Whether it's a vision board in your bedroom or a checklist on the fridge, we need reminders. I used to have a card stuck on the inside of my wallet — a prompt every single time I opened it up to pay for something. "Is this a need?" Today, if I had one, I might amend it with a focus on my happiness and it would say, "Is this in line with my values?"

Antonio Rangel, professor of neuroscience and economics at the California Institute of Technology, put people in front of a computer and displayed choices: $20 now, $50 in six months, $80 in a year and so on. He manipulated how long the test subjects fixated on the different options, increasing the probability that they'd choose the one he wanted. "Imagine when you are at the buffet table and every time you had to make a choice, someone put flashing neon lights:

healthy, healthy, healthy!" he told me. It doesn't mean that you're going to always choose the healthy option. But if you pay more attention to the signs you put out there, on average, are you going to make better choices? Probably.

YOUR HAPPY MONEY TO-DO LIST

- Write your SMART goals down and consider breaking them into micro-goals. Tell a friend, your mom, your OHM tribe. Check in regularly.
- Ask a friend what her money goals are. Ask her how you can help her achieve them.
- Challenge your friends to a month-long money contest. Maybe it's a savings challenge. See if you can limit your spending to an agreed-upon amount every week and post your progress on a Facebook group.
- Choose a date one year or years from now (an anniversary or birthday). Imagine that your money journey has gone well and things have turned out wonderfully. Write yourself a short letter, telling yourself about how life is going and what you did to get there.

MONEY TALKS

- What motivates you when it comes to goals or challenges?
- Describe a goal you achieved and how you got there. Could you apply any of the same strategies to a monetary goal?
- What have you tried in the past that has worked for managing your money?

HAPPINESS FOR LATER

*Saving strategies and investment savvy that
will have you laughing all the way to the bank.*

16
SAVE RIGHT

Here's a typical morning: I'm late. I'm wrestling clothes onto my toddler in the doorway then launching all of our gear into the backseat of our SUV like it's a garbage truck. At his school, he's pulling me down the hallway like I'm a donkey, laden with his backpack, nap-time pillow and blanket, lunch bag, snow suit, etc. Then I'm driving home because I forgot his winter boots for recess, and I'm doing a conference call over speakerphone. I duck into a coffee shop to answer emails and do some writing on deadline, and I'm suddenly aware that I'm wearing a pyjama shirt and jeans. (I need to invest in outfits that will go from day to night to day again.)

I also blurt to myself, "Oh man, I forgot to brush my face today!" which means I forgot to brush my teeth and wash my face. The day is a blur. I pick up the kid and go to the grocery store to shop for dinner.

Now at this point, while my son alternates between wanting to see the lobster tank and whining for a cupcake, I'm supposed to make smart money choices. I'm supposed to walk the bright aisles filled with pick-me-uppers and make good decisions: do I want to save $30 for his college fund or spend $30 on cheese? Just point me to the wine.

It is hard to make the choice to save money on a daily basis. That's a lot of pressure. Yes, I know, and I'm sure by now you do too, that delaying gratification can boost happiness. It spreads out the happiness. Some happiness now. Some happiness later. The motivated, best version of me knows this and will make the right decisions. But she's not always around.

We have to make it easier for ourselves to save.

Make it automatic

Saving needs to become a habit. It's like a muscle. The more you use it, the more it'll become part of your routine and the easier it will be.

If you need to, start small. We don't start at the gym with the heaviest dumbbells. Start by saving an innocuous amount. Maybe every time you get a $5 bill, put it in a jar or envelope for your emergency fund or your travel stash or your holiday gift reserve. Start with whatever you can. Ten dollars a week. Twenty-five. If you start with $100 a month, one day, $500 or $1,000 won't make you as unhappy because your savings muscle will already be well defined. That being said, if you want a Mr. Universe–worthy bank account, it pays to be more aggressive with your savings.

A lot of us default to saving our leftovers. We wait until

the end of the month, after money has been sucked away for rent or mortgages or insurance or car payments or debt interest payments, and whatever's leftover goes toward our longer-term goals.

I liken this to me with a bowl of chips. At the start, I think, "I need to save some of this crunchtastic salty goodness for tomorrow." Ten minutes later, I'm daubing at crumbs with a moistened index finger.

You need to put aside a handful of chips *before* you start eating. This sounds like we're admitting defeat. Like we can't count on our future selves to be disciplined. But, as I said, saving is hard. For everyone. Most people are not active savers. We have as much eagerness about boosting savings as we do about peeling potatoes or meeting the new girlfriend's parents.

If you set up a system where money is automatically transferred from your chequing account into a savings/investment account, you won't be tempted to spend what isn't available. I promise that you won't even notice that it's gone. Do it biweekly to coincide with payday. Go do it right now. If you already do this, consider bumping up the contribution or setting up another one.

Often, the more you make, the more you spend. So, if you get that much-deserved raise, before you've had time to adjust to your new higher income lifestyle, automatically sock that extra money away by upping your savings with the amount of your raise.

If you're self-employed and automatic saving makes you nervous — what if money comes out during a dry spell and you need that money to cover rent? — try just a small amount. If you're uncomfortable with this, consider saving a percentage of every cheque that you receive. (You should be doing this anyway because the government is going to be coming for its cut at the end of the year.)

Your automatic savings plan takes money out of your chequing account. And, if you remember from our chat about budgeting, you can also make an automatic transfer of money from your chequing account to your spending account. If there's money in my spending account, I'm buying the wine *and* the cheese — and a lobster and cupcake for my kid.

SOME FOR ME AND SOME FOR ME

Here's a way to help you save while you spend. Some banks allow you to round up or set an amount to be added to each debit card transaction. TD Canada Trust has a program called Simply Save. Every time you buy something with your debit card, a set amount from $0.50 to $5 is automatically transferred to your savings account. Meanwhile, Bank of America has Keep the Change, which allows you to round up your purchases to the next dollar and the difference goes into your savings account. A number of spare change investing apps have popped up, including Acorns and Mylo, where the purchases can be rounded up and the difference automatically invested. Set it up, forget about it and accumulate money in a separate account to cover your anniversary dinners or charitable donations.

Nice figure

When it comes to long-term savings, we inevitably ask how much we need to save.

Financial planning company LearnVe$t suggests using the 50/30/20 rule: 50% of your pay should go to essentials (housing, food), 30% should go to lifestyle choices (entertainment, travel) and 20% should go to money priorities (retirement contributions, emergency savings, tackling debt, etc.).

Bleh. I don't enjoy rules of thumb. Applying general formulas to our savings strategies is as accurate as taking a magazine personality quiz. (If you're living rent-free with your parents, for example, you can save a lot more than 20% for your money priorities.) Also, sometimes these rules of thumb can become outdated, without us realizing it.

But if you can save 20% of your take-home pay, that's good. Ten to 15% is good too — it's much more than the average household is saving. (Households in Canada and the U.S. have been saving less than 6% in recent years.) If you have big, fabulous goals, like early retirement or a year-long trip to fund, then you'll need to be saving more — at least 50%.

If you heard that everyone could stand to lose exactly 10 pounds to be healthier, you'd call bullshit, look at your own circumstances and estimate a number that works for your life and your plans. How much do we need to save? *It depends.*

How much should you save in an emergency fund? A minimum of three months' worth of living expenses or more? Well, it depends. Are you a full-time permanent government employee, or are you a freelance musician?

How much should you save for retirement? Many experts say between 10% and 15% of your earnings, starting in your

20s. But, oh, it really depends. Are you 25 or 45 years old? Do you live in a small town or the big city? Do you have a magical defined contribution pension? When will you leave your job in a blaze of glory? And will you die at 72 or rock it until you're 102?

Argh. This is why people look for rules of thumb. To make for shorter reading. We'll get to a number more tailored to your needs soon.

Thinking of how much you'll need to have saved can be daunting, overwhelming. Establish bite-sized milestones, such as getting to that first $1,000. Figure out how long it will take to get there and do whatever you can to get to that first stepping stone. Achieving those milestones is much more plausible than deciding to save a million bucks for retirement; that feels unfathomable. But we're builders and we'll do it one brick at a time. Just focus on the bricks. Or approach it like that cake in the fridge. We know the cake will get eaten. One bite at a time.

The money miracle

It's been called magical. A miracle. The eighth wonder of the world. You'd think it's a monkey's paw that grants monetary wishes or a genuine Nigerian prince who is leaving you an inheritance, but nope, I'm talking about compounding interest.

Your brain may have just played the sad trombone noise, but my brain popped fireworks.

What exactly is compounding interest, and why is it magical for your bank account? Think of it as interest on interest. It's interest on your initial principal (your original investment) and then on the accumulated interest. Doesn't sound like something that deserves a parade, but it is.

Its power is like the Force. Depending on how it is used, the power can be good or evil. It can be your friend or your enemy depending on whether you earn it or you pay it.

For your savings, time can turn compounding interest into your BFF. This friendship grows and grows over the years. It starts as this little baby lizard cradled in the crook of your arm, and then one day it's a massive dragon able to help you fulfill your destiny and conquer lands. Let's say you invested $1,000 and it earned 5% in interest last year. Today, you'd be earning interest on $1,050. Now, let's say you invested $1,000 in the bank and left it to grow for 30 years with a 5% rate of return, compounded annually; even if you never added any more money, you'd have more than $4,300.

Without time, your dragon will not grow to its full potential. (To describe the phenomenon that is compounding interest, I'm using a dragon metaphor. In my news articles, I use gremlins growing in a pool of water; fellow finance author Robert R. Brown uses zombies and horny rabbits — one zombie bites another zombie who bites more; one rabbit bones another rabbit to make 10 more who bone 10 more and so on.)

Dragons, gremlins, zombies and bunnies aside, let's use the example of two Melissas to illustrate the importance of starting to save as early as possible. Both Melissas have $1,000 a year to invest for a certain period of time. Melissa A starts early, when she's 20, and stops when she's 34. Melissa B starts saving at 30 years old (her 20s were for concerts and travel and bottle service and definitely not saving). She puts $1,000 every year into her savings account until she's 64. Both make 6% annually on their investments. Who ends up with more?

	Melissa A	Melissa B
Age when she started investing	20	30
Age when she stopped investing	34	64
Total amount invested by age 65	$15,000	$35,000
Who wins?	$141,700	$118,000

Melissa B started late but invested more. Melissa A, who stopped saving a few years after her doppelgänger began, comes out on top. That's the magic of compounding interest over time.

Even if you feel like Melissa B, don't despair. First, you're equally as attractive as Melissa A. Second, you can make up for the time lost with some smart strategies. Just don't wait any longer.

THE RULE OF 72

I hate math. I said it. I was an honour roll student with braces, big glasses and a poodle perm, but despite the dorky clichés and the dumb-ass racial stereotype about Asians, I shudder at numbers. Mofo will catch me trying to tally something, my face scrunched, my fingers wiggling, and he'll make fun of my "hand abacus."

But the rule of 72 is easy math. It's a short-cut that will tell you approximately how long an investment will take to double.

The formula: 72 / Interest rate = Years it'll take to double.

If you invest your money at a 6% rate of return, your money will take 12 years to double (72/6 = 12).

If you want to double your money in 10 years, you need a 7.2% rate of return (72/7.2 = 10).

Rate of Return	Rule of 72
2%	36.0
3%	24.0
5%	14.4
7%	10.3
9%	8.0
12%	6.0
25%	2.9

YOUR HAPPY MONEY TO-DO LIST

- Set up an automatic savings plan for any specific goal. Or if you already have one, bump it up.
- Look into any incentives or programs through your bank that might help you save more money.

MONEY TALKS
- What is your biggest impediment to saving?
- What's the most important thing you want to do with your money in the next five years? Ten years?

17
MAKE THAT MONEY WORK

When I took a financial securities course, one of the most painful things I learned was calculating bond values. So, that's what we're going to do right now. Just kidding. As I said, math equations are the antipode to my joy.

When we talk about financial smarts, a lot of people assume that means investing savvy. Then they (mostly men) inevitably try to talk to me about bitcoin and stock picks and foreign exchange trading. Sure, understanding the concepts and knowing the lingo helps, but that's not what determines your money success. (It starts with spending less than you make, consistently saving and then taking protective measures.) But I want to share a bit about investments to help your savings grow and grow. For the record, I wiped my memory of how to compute bond values so don't even ask.

There's a bewildering number of investment choices out there from stocks to real estate to cryptocurrencies to He-Man figurines. And as much as I love the Masters of the Universe, I'm going to focus next on the time-tested strategies of building wealth in the stock market.

Yes, in the stock market, your investments could shrink; we all recall 2008 when the world's stocks reportedly lost 48%. You can't prevent your investment portfolio from getting hit with temporary losses, but there are ways to avoid getting clobbered in downturns: determine your risk tolerance, consider your time horizon and diversify.

Determine your risk tolerance: The riskier the investment, typically the higher the potential return. (The operative word there is "potential.") The rule of thumb is that in your 20s and 30s, you can handle riskier investments because you have time to ride out the inevitable dives in the market. (This is compared to people who are nearing retirement and need to cash out their nest-egg money to live on for 20 to 30 years.) But this doesn't account for how squeamish you are about losing your money. You have to be honest with yourself about whether you can stomach a loss. Will you pop a vein in your head from anxiety when your investments fall? If you're extremely risk averse, consider this: stocks go up and they go down, but historically the market has trended upward. So if you've invested for the long term (20 years and more), you'll likely see growth. Finance website NerdWallet ran 10,000 possible scenarios for investors, based on historical S&P 500 (a basket of stocks issued by 500 large American companies) and treasury returns. A 25-year-old earning $40,456 (adjusted annually for inflation) and investing 15% each year has more than a 99% chance of maintaining at least their initial investment over 40 years. But more importantly, investors also had a 95% chance of earning nearly three times their initial investment — that's at least $1.67 million. (They had a 75% chance of earning at least $3.14 million.) Absolutely, past performance is not an indicator of future performance. But if you've got time, you can afford to be riskier.

Consider your time horizon: If you need your money in fewer than five years, put it in safer investments. (Think of scenarios where you might need that money. For example, will you need to sell investments if you lose your job in the near future? What if the market is in one of its periodic slumps? Will you be okay with taking a hit?) If you're in for the long haul, you can opt for riskier investments. The long haul is what your dragon needs.

Diversify: Essentially, don't put all of your eggs into one basket, don't bet it all on one horse, don't swipe right on just one guy. In the stock market, this means choosing stocks or funds in more than one sector (financials versus energy, for example) and investing at home and abroad. This means having a mix in your portfolio of stocks, bonds and cash. You could also create a diversified portfolio with a handful of mutual funds or index funds or exchange-traded funds.

WTF (what the finance)
If all of this investing talk is to you like mumble rap to me (what the what is coming out of her mouth?!?), here's a quick breakdown of the key kinds of investments you can buy.

Stocks: Super simply, a stock is a small piece of a company. To raise money, companies issue shares and sell them to the general public. The shares or stock can then be traded on a market like the New York Stock Exchange.

YAY: Investing in stocks can give you high returns. From 1928 to 2016, the S&P 500 earned about 10% per year. Also, some companies dole out a portion of their earnings to shareholders in cash through something called a dividend; in other words, the company is paying you to own its stock. Bonus!

BOO: Sure, stocks can rise sharply, but they can also plummet. The market has had stretches of blah returns and times of bad losses. So stocks can be volatile in the short term.

Bonds: A bond is like an IOU. When you buy a bond, you're lending your money to a company or a government (the issuer). The period of the loan can be months to as long as 30 years. The issuer pays you interest. And when the period is done (the maturity date), the issuer pays you back the face value of the bond (what they originally borrowed from you). Bond prices fluctuate. If the price of your bond goes up after you've bought it, you can make money by selling it before it matures.

YAY: Bonds provide diversification in your portfolio. Also, when stocks drop in a crappy economic environment, bonds may go up in value.

BOO: If you sell your bond for less than you paid, you could lose money. Your issuer could get into money trouble and be unable to pay you interest or even pay back the initial investment. Also, your returns might not keep pace with inflation.

Guaranteed investment certificates: GICs pay a higher interest rate than savings accounts because they typically tie up your money for a period between 90 days and 10 years. The bank agrees to pay you a guaranteed amount as long as you don't withdraw your money early. If you do, you could forfeit any interest if it only gets paid on the maturity date, and you could face a penalty. A cashable or redeemable GIC, however, lets you take your cash out at any time without getting dinged.

YAY: No fees to buy. Guaranteed return. This could play an important part of your diversified portfolio.

BOO: The modest returns from your GIC will likely not compete with stock market returns. In some cases, it might not even beat inflation.

Mutual funds: A mutual fund is like a box of chocolates. But instead of caramels and pralines, you have stocks, bonds or other securities. A bunch of investors (maybe including you) pool their money to buy this box of chocolates, and a portfolio manager manages it, sometimes switching out the treats for other tastier ones. There are more than 15,000 chocolate boxes . . . er, mutual funds in North America, but different funds have varying risks and expected returns. You can take a DIY approach and buy them yourself, but mostly mutual funds are sold to you by brokers and advisors who provide a financial planning service to you in exchange for fund fees.

YAY: Ideal for novice investors who want diversification and advice from a financial advisor.

BOO: Mutual fund fees can be high. (A fee of 2.5% of the total invested in the fund is common.) This means your fund has to perform better than average to be a worthwhile commitment of your cash.

Index funds: Index funds are mutual funds, but they hold all of the stocks or bonds on an index. (An index is just a list of investments.) So again it's like a box of chocolates, but the box is filled with chocolates on a specific dessert list. So rather than you, for example, buying all 500 stocks featured on the S&P 500 index, you're basically buying a fund or bundle of stocks that replicates the movement of the S&P 500.

YAY: Index funds generally cost less than actively managed mutual funds. And lots of index funds do not have fees when shares are bought or sold. They're still good for regular savers with a starting portfolio, and you can buy them yourself by opening an account with an online brokerage.

BOO: When someone says the market is up or down, they're usually talking about an index. Index funds follow the movement of the market. So when there are downs in the market, your index funds also go down.

Exchange-traded funds: ETFs also track an index. They typically have even lower fees than mutual funds and index funds. You can purchase them yourself by opening an account with an online brokerage such as Questrade, or an advisor can recommend and build a portfolio for you. Some platforms combine these services: online investment manager Wealthsimple, for example, asks you a bunch of questions, develops an investment strategy for you and uses your money to buy a diversified mix of ETFs.

YAY: Low, low cost. Fees are a fraction of those charged for similar mutual funds.

BOO: ETFs are traded like stocks. You may pay a trading fee each time you invest money, so if you're investing a small amount and trading often, it might not be worth it. It's also easier for a novice to find a financial advisor who will sell them mutual funds.

LOW-STRESS INVESTING

I'm not a sports fan. I can't take the stress of watching, my insides wrung like a towel. (Researchers looked at data from hospitals around Munich during the 2006 World Cup games and found that viewing a stressful soccer match more than doubles your risk of having a minor cardiovascular event.) I also can't take the stress of looking at my investments every day — the wins, the losses, the in between . . . all in a day. To minimize stress, follow these three investing tips.

1. Don't constantly check your investments.

Okay, maybe you're the type of person who gets off on watching the stock market rise. (Okay, *now* I'm done using erotic references in this book.) And then when the market falls, you're also thrilled because now the stocks are "on sale" and you're betting that they won't continue to plummet. But if you're like me, you don't need the drama. I'd rather set it and forget it. Here's all you need to do:

- Check in on your investments once or twice a year.
- Add to your portfolio and rebalance to the appropriate weighting (for example, 20% bonds, 80% stocks — more on this later) on a set schedule, which will reduce your risk of emotional buying or selling.
- Talk with your advisor at least once a year.

Looking at it every week could stress you out. The market goes up and it goes down. You don't need to look every day to see if your dragon has sprouted a whisker. It's magic — it changes moment to moment, but it needs time to grow.

2. Don't constantly buy and sell investments.

My colleague and finance guru Preet Banerjee says that investments are like soap: the more you touch them, the smaller they get. Sure, I get the adage "buy low, sell high" — but we almost always miss the top or bottom. The most successful investors buy and hold for the long term. Finance professors Terrance Odean and Brad Barber have published a series of studies, including one 2000 paper entitled "Trading is hazardous to your wealth"; they analyzed 66,465 accounts at a large discount brokerage firm and found that those who traded the most had reduced returns.

3. Invest with a conscience.

For your investment portfolio, consider including securities that reflect your values. For example, CoPower Green Bonds uses your investment to help fund clean energy initiatives across North America. There are also a number of socially responsible ETFs out there. For example, the ETF listed as HERS replicates the performance of a list of companies committed to gender diversity and workplace inclusion. Wealthsimple users can simply check a box to choose a socially responsible portfolio.

Savings on steroids . . . or Viagra (if we want to quote my mom)

There are some things I'll never understand. Like why a guy friend would send Mofo a poop pic for laughs. Or why people who have the means ignore programs that offer free money for your savings. When the government gives a grant or my employer offers to match my retirement contributions, it's like someone offering to supersize my fries. My answer is always "Hell yes." But reports show that people are not taking advantage of employer-sponsored retirement plans such as 401(k)s. Get on that magic unicorn.

If it's important to you to save for your kid's education, there are great tools at your disposal. In the U.S., you have the 529 plan, a savings plan with awesome tax benefits. The earnings on your investment grow tax-free inside this account, and you can withdraw the funds tax-free just as long as you spend the money on qualified education expenses (tuition, computers, room and board, etc.). On top of that, some states offer full or partial tax deductions for contributions.

For Canadians, there's no greater deal out there than the registered educations savings plan. It's similar to the 529 plan, where your investment gains are not taxed; however, when you withdraw the money, the money is taxed in the hands of the beneficiary (your kids). But — this is the best — the Canadian government gives you free money. Contribute at least $2,500 a year to get the maximum federal government grant of $500 (the government matches 20% of the first $2,500 contributed each year for eligible children to a lifetime limit of $7,200). To be eligible for the grant, you have to start saving for your kid's RESP before the end of the year of their 15th birthday. FREE MONEY! Parents, run, don't walk, to a bank to open up an education savings plan if you haven't already.

Put your savings in your house

I'm not talking about stashing all of your cash under your mattress. And yes, I know someone who actually does that. No, I can't tell you where he lives.

Your primary residence is a tax-free investment — as in you're not taxed on the appreciation in the value of your home. Putting money toward the mortgage is another form of forced savings. By paying down your mortgage, you are increasing your net worth.

Some people say, "Meh, with interest rates so low, I'm putting my money into other investments." Fair. But consider two things. Some people, like Mofo and me, feel uncomfortable having large debt, including house debt. Secondly, interest rates won't always be so low. In Canada, where mortgages can come up for renewal every few years, you could be facing higher rates at renewal time. Low interest rates are a gift to us because they provide an opportunity to pay down as much principal as possible in these early years when interest eats up most of the payments. With your 25-year amortization (fancy word for repayment schedule), you still could end up paying hundreds of thousands of dollars in interest to the bank over that term. Here are a few ways to pay off your house faster.

- Shorten your amortization. Say you take out a $250,000 mortgage at a 4.99% interest rate on a fixed term with monthly payments:

Amortization	Approx. total interest paid
30	$229,000
20	$185,000

- Increase the frequency of your payments. Make accelerated biweekly or weekly payments instead of monthly. They will amount to one extra monthly payment. Over 25 years, that extra payment to the principal adds up. Say you have a $250,000 mortgage at 3.79% interest:

Payment frequency	Approx. years to pay it off
Monthly payments	25
Biweekly payments	22*
*(saving you almost $20,000 in interest)	

- Dump a lump sum directly onto the principal. Most mortgages allow you to make an extra payment every year, sometimes on your mortgage anniversary date, so drop a money bomb to take out some of that house debt. Where does one get such a money bomb? Maybe a work bonus, an inheritance, birthday money or a tax refund?

- Top up your mortgage payments. Some mortgages allow you to top up your regular instalments, which goes directly to the principal. Take a $250,000 mortgage with a five-year fixed term at a rate of 4.99%, amortized over 25 years. If the payment was topped up by $150 a month, you'd save four years and $35,000 in interest.

Before you dump every last cent you have into your mortgage, keep in mind that you run the risk of being house rich and cash poor. (You're putting money into something that can't be accessed if you readily need it.) Think about your other savings priorities (emergency fund, retirement) and short-term plans (glamping at a music festival, wiping out debt) before putting it all in your house. Also consider that your extra cash could be going to your dragon, which might be more valuable.

If you want more opportunities for the future, then you have to make choices and manage your money in a way that will give you that. After Mofo and I got married, we bought a sliver of a townhouse even though climbing three flights of stairs felt like I was running to the top of a lighthouse every day. The bedrooms were triangular and the halls so narrow that we had to move our furniture in through a second-storey patio door. It was in the boonies even though I had vowed never to leave the city core. But we wanted children one day, and we hoped Mofo would stay at home with them while I returned to work. This home, we could afford on one income. It was the house that allowed us to save a ton of money for later. And it was the house that sheltered us through Mofo's mental storm.

SO YOU WANT TO BE A LANDLORD?

Mofo and I have two rental properties. I need another book — or a sitcom — to share the adventures of buying investment properties and being a landlord. We've learned so much. If I could send a letter back through time to myself as I embarked on this journey, it would go like this:

Dear Melissa,

The perfect tenant is like a leprechaun. They'll mind your pot of real estate gold at the end of a happy rainbow, but they can be hard to find. You'll have to go on the hunt for the perfect tenant every year or so. Be discerning. Get credit and employment information. Ask a bagillion questions. Stalk them online. Some prospects may look like leprechauns, but they're really horrible trolls. Remember that the law favours tenants, and trying to evict one will make you more familiar with a courtroom than the cast of Law & Order. *Do everything you can to avoid that nightmare. Even if someone checks all the financial boxes, that doesn't mean they're all rainbows and Lucky Charms. For example, you'll rent to a sweet, retired grandmother. But she'll call you every time she smells marijuana while sitting on her balcony.*

Now, some tenants seem like leprechauns but after they've moved out, you realize that they were just green . . . like the Hulk. And Hulk smash. They store food in a rage, you surmise, given all the broken drawers in the fridge. They drag furniture around the hardwood, using coffee tables like Spirographs. They cultivate black mould farms in brand-new washing machines. It's infuriating — perplexing (how does a five-foot med student wiggle loose a toilet?) — but you are responsible for fixing things. And for paying to fix things. Take this into account when running your numbers.

Run the numbers for a bunch of scenarios. But remember, the money part doesn't always work out. Condo fees or property taxes could spike. Extended vacancy periods could arise. Unexpected costs come up every year — an air-conditioning unit will need fixing, a dryer will need replacing. Always have a cushion of cash to cover shortfalls. Always have an exit strategy. You'll consider selling, but it might not be the right time in the market — plus real estate and legal fees are costly.

Being a landlord is not for everyone, but it's for you. Mofo loves investing in real estate because it's a tangible investment, and he gets to play an active role in how it performs. Both of your rental properties will appreciate in value. One will take about a decade to be paid off — and it will be paid for by renters. You'll enjoy added monthly income after covering all of your costs. While you'll get taxed on this income, you can deduct your expenses (including mortgage interest, insurance and maintenance).

It's magically delicious.

YOUR HAPPY MONEY TO-DO LIST

- Familiarize yourself with the types of investments out there. If you already have investments, find out what you've invested your money in.

- Make an appointment to talk to an advisor at your bank about investments or look into a robo-advisor (an online portfolio management service) such as Wealthfront or Wealthsimple. Consider opening an account with a discount brokerage like TD Ameritrade or Questrade to trade your own investment products.

- Determine how long you expect to invest your money. Think about your attitude about risk. Online surveys, such as the one provided by investment company Vanguard, can help you consider your time horizon and risk tolerance and how this relates to the kinds of investments in your portfolio.

- Look into the rules of your mortgage. Do they allow for lump sum payments or top-ups? Call your mortgage company or bank to switch your schedule from monthly to biweekly instalments.

- Consider whether buying and managing an investment property is for you. Do you want to be a landlord? Can you afford it? You'll need at least a 20% down payment to buy a property and money to cover ongoing costs and unexpected expenses. Would you need to hire a property manager, and how much would that cost? Do as much research as possible before jumping in.

MONEY TALKS

- One of your investments loses 15% of its value shortly after you buy it. Do you sell it, hold on and wait or buy more of the same investment?
- If you invested $10,000, would you rather experience very little market fluctuation to make $10,400, some fluctuation to make $11,000 or a lot of fluctuation to make $13,000?
- You've just hit the $25,000 level in a game show. Do you take the money and run or bet it all with a 50% chance of doubling your money?

18
MAKE THE SILVER FOX HAPPY

Imagine for a moment future you.

You look good. And you're still kicking ass like a Denzel Washington or a Meryl Streep. You're not working anymore but you're still so busy — you've got grandkids to spoil, cruises to sail, girlfriends/boyfriends to smooch . . .

Now in terms of funds, what does future you need to be over-the-moon happy?

This exercise is important. "To people estranged from their future selves, saving is like a choice between spending money today or giving it to a stranger years from now," U.S. researchers wrote in a 2011 study published in the *Journal of Marketing Research*. The scientists showed people aged renderings of themselves. They found that the people were willing to allocate about 30% more of their pay to retirement than those who had not seen their "future selves."

"It's almost like an imagination aid to give people something to grasp onto and make them realize, one day you will be in retirement. That person who will ultimately end up being you is dependent on the choices you make now," says Hal Hershfield, one of the lead authors of the study and a marketing professor at UCLA's Anderson School of Management. (So that Snapchat filter that makes you into a grandma could have a significant impact on your future happiness.)

For many of us, retirement is this big, amorphous faraway thing that is overwhelming to think about. It brings to my mind old folks' homes and tennis visors and pink sweatsuits. But that's not how life is in later years for everyone. It's not how I envision my retirement anyway (well, maybe the pink sweatsuits). I picture it more like Cher's 2017 Billboard Music Awards performance where the 71-year-old music legend turned back time in strategically placed sequins, bling and sheer body-stockings. When I'm 71, I want to still be doing great work and looking fabulous in whatever the eff I want.

I want three things: I want to be doing the work of my choosing — whether that's becoming a mime or writing Star Wars fan fiction or being a nanny to my grandkids — and this may or may not pay the bills. I want the freedom to explore warmer climates while my neighbours are shovelling snow. Finally, I want the peace of mind of knowing that I'm covered. If I'm not as healthy, if I never make another cent, if I live to be 101, I'm good. I've never been one to rely on others to take care of me (and the government and its pension will not be enough to cover us).

I have to plan for this. You have to plan for this. You're

a fox now, but one day you'll be a silver fox. And Silver Fox deserves to be happy too.

Get Silver Fox's number

As I've said before, I wouldn't ride or die by any savings rules. But they can be motivating guidelines. Let me share three guidelines with you, and you can choose one that resonates with you.

Finance guru Suze Orman says you should save 15% of your pre-tax income for retirement and then 25% when you hit your 40s. (That means if you're in your 20s or 30s and you make $50,000 a year, then you should be saving $7,500 a year or $625 a month.)

Asset management firm Fidelity uses this rule for retirement savings: save at least 10 times your ending salary by age 67. Try to have at least as much as your current salary saved by 30. Two times your salary saved by 35, then at least four times by 45. (Fidelity analysts assume you started saving 15% at age 25, will retire at 67 and will live until you're 92.)

Russell Investments Canada has the retirement rule of $25. For every $1 of annual income you'll need in retirement, you'll need 25 times saved. For example, if you want $20,000 a year in retirement, you'll need $500,000 in registered savings, based on average life expectancies (79 for men and 83 for women).

Most retirement plans assume that you're going to live off 70% of your income at retirement: if your pre-retirement salary was $100,000, you'll get by with $70,000. Keep the costs of your current lifestyle in mind as a start, but hopefully your house will be paid off and the kids will have moved out (unless they're like Mofo or my little sister — then prepare to cook your gigantic babies dinner forever) so you'll have fewer expenses. Online retirement calculators can also help you come up with a number more tailored to your age, income and circumstances. They may include what you'll receive from the government (the Canada Pension Plan and Old Age Security, or Social Security retirement benefits in the U.S.). If you're in your 40s and you have nothing saved for retirement, hit the accelerator: you can still reach your goals.

And remember whatever amount you can save a month for Silver Fox, just make it automatic; do it online, or call your advisor or mutual fund broker to set up a monthly withdrawal into your Canadian TFSA or RRSP, or in the U.S., your Roth IRA or your individual retirement account (IRA).

Fill your bags with good stuff

Your 401(k), traditional IRA, Roth IRA, TFSA, RRSP are like bags. You put money in them. Then you invest the money into different investment products such as mutual funds, exchange-traded funds, guarantee investment certificates, stocks or bonds.

You're playing the long game. Your goal is to leave the money to grow for decades, so your risk tolerance is going to be different than if you needed the money next year. You'll want a diverse mix of stuff in the bag.

As a starting point, consider this rule of thumb: subtract your age from 100 and put that percentage of your retirement savings in stocks while the rest goes into safer investments like fixed income products such as bonds and guaranteed investment certificates. So if you're 30, 70% of your money would be in stocks. If you feel comfortable taking a little more risk, subtract your age from 110.

Silver Fox will stop working. And she will need money to live. Because of the magic of compounding interest, it is smarter for you to start putting money away for her today than to wait a decade. Consider this metaphor: in the event of emergency, flight attendants tell you to put on your oxygen mask before helping others. You have to take care of you first. When applying this metaphor to your money, you might think, "Okay, take care of me first and then take care of Silver Fox." That's wrong. Silver Fox is *you*. Take care of you first. Ahead of your kid's education savings. Ahead of your family vacation fund. Make yourself — and your retirement savings — a top priority.

FREQUENTLY ASKED QUESTIONS THAT SILVER FOX WILL BE GLAD YOU ASKED

I have no money for Silver Fox. Should I borrow money to fund my retirement?

In my early 20s, before the TFSA existed in Canada, before I had a mortgage or any other major responsibilities, I wanted to get a jump start on my retirement savings. I had not been saving throughout the year, so I borrowed the funds to make an RRSP contribution. I had no other debt and I felt confident that I would repay the loan within six to eight months. I also used 100% of my tax refund to pay down part of the loan. However, I wasn't in a high tax bracket so there wasn't much of a tax advantage.

Would I suggest that people borrow to fund their retirement?

In the majority of cases, no. I did it because I made the mistake of not saving in the first place. So, my advice is don't make my original mistake of not saving. Or if you haven't saved, consider contributing what you would have paid to service the loan every month. I believe if you don't have money, you generally shouldn't borrow it. (More on that later.) And are you starting a cycle of needing loans every year just to make a contribution?

Rather than adding more debt to your plate, we should be reducing it because the goal is to retire debt-free.

Should I borrow from my retirement fund to buy my first home?

In my mid- to late 20s, I raided my retirement account to buy a condo unit pre-construction. The Canadian government's Home Buyers' Plan enables you to borrow up to $25,000 tax-free from your RRSP to buy your first home. The amount must be repaid within 15 years. The IRS allows first-time homebuyers to withdraw a lifetime limit of $10,000 from their IRAs without penalty — but you pay income tax on withdrawals.

I had previously lived alone downtown or with roommates. At my previous apartment, we had fought a traumatizing war against bedbugs. Speaking of traumatizing, one afternoon, someone broke through our front door, presumably to rob us. My best friend who was asleep in my room called out, and the intruder fled. I wanted a place of my own.

I bought a $189,000 one-bedroom unit, based off a floor plan, plus a $24,000 parking space. I had more than $30,000 as a down payment and my parents gifted me $10,000. (I had already maxed out my RRSP contributions, but if I had had the room, I could've put that $10,000 gift into the RRSP to get a refund.)

At the time, I was grateful that I could afford to buy my home in this way. I lived there for five glorious years until I got married.

Looking back today, however, I understand what I traded. I gave my baby dragon away to buy a home. The point of the retirement savings account is to hatch your dragon and let the decades turn it into a monstrous beast. I went into my nest and stole it before the monster had enough time to mew, let alone roar. Back then, I was only allowed to take $20,000 through the Home Buyers' Plan, but that was a good thing.

I can't say that I regret the decision. But I'm sure Silver Fox would disagree. All I can do now is everything I can to make up for it.

Woohoo! I got money! What should I spend my tax refund on? Experiences, time savers or gifts for others?

I know what I said, but no, no, no. Spending your retirement contribution on travel or furniture might make you happy today, but it will make the

Silver Fox miserable. It's not free money. It's your money. It's Silver Fox's money. You need a smart strategy for your refund, whether it's investing it, paying down debt or mortgage or putting it back into your retirement fund.

Knowing that you're taking care of your future self will give you peace and satisfaction. You need to make sure Silver Fox has everything she needs. She may not want to downsize and live in a condo. She may need more in terms of health-care costs, or she may find an elixir and live longer than anyone ever imagined. Make sure she/you will be happy because she/you will have choices.

Should I pay down debt, or should I save and invest?

All debt isn't created equal. If you have credit card debt, for example, turn on your beast mode and attack it. Do that ahead of saving for Silver Fox. (More on debt coming up.)

On the other hand, it might not make sense to tackle your mortgage or a student loan, which have low-interest rates, over investing in your TFSA. Your investments could get a greater return than what you're paying in interest on your debts. And if you're younger, remember your dragon and the story of the two beautiful Melissas. Starting early matters.

Something else to think about? If you're in a higher tax bracket, it might be important to reduce the tax you pay. If you think you'll be in a lower tax bracket in retirement, make an RRSP contribution instead of paying down debt — especially if your company matches contributions. You could also use your tax refund to pay down debt.

YOUR HAPPY MONEY TO-DO LIST

- Visit an online retirement calculator and plug in some numbers to get an idea of how much Silver Fox will need to enjoy life.
- If you don't have a traditional IRA, Roth IRA, RRSP or TFSA, contact your bank or a financial advisor or look into robo-advisors such as Wealthsimple. Ask if they have any incentives for opening an account. (For example, I've seen some promotions where you'll get 15% of your first month's contribution.) Ask friends for advice and, when possible, referral codes.
- Canadians should check their notices of assessment from the CRA to see the RRSP contribution room, and Americans should check in with the IRA's annual contribution limit and look out for catch-up contribution room for those over 50.
- Set up a monthly automatic withdrawal to your retirement accounts.
- Does your company have a group retirement plan? Email your human resources rep ASAP and ask if you're taking full advantage of the plan's benefits.
- Spend some time looking into your investment options. Try to understand your own investment

needs; identify your time horizon and your risk tolerance. If you already have a financial advisor, set up your annual meeting and prepare a list of questions to ask them about your investments.

- If you're getting a tax refund, commit to yourself, to your OHM tribe, to Silver Fox, that you will put it toward a money smart goal.

MONEY TALKS

- If you had a hot tub time machine, what would you say to yourself about money at 65 years old? What do you think your 65-year-old self would say to you?
- Name a Silver Fox that you admire or relate to and explain why.
- Imagine your life in retirement. How do you spend your days? Do you travel? Where do you live? What kind of work or volunteering do you do?

19
HOOKING UP WITH A FINANCIAL ADVISOR

There's no shame in asking for help when it comes to your savings goals. We might hire a personal trainer to keep our squat forms from being knock-kneed and hunched. We might seek out a marriage counsellor to help convince our partners that we're always right. And we might need a professional to help us achieve our money goals and keep us accountable (yes, your OHM tribe or your mom might not be enough).

I often hear people say that they'd love to work with a financial advisor but they're waiting until they have more money put aside or until their debt is paid off. That's like saying you'll hire a running coach after completing your first marathon. Your financial advisor will help you with your goals.

Your relationship with your financial advisor is a special one. This person is going to know things about you that even your partner or parents might not know. This person is going to be the keeper of your dreams and desires. (Just so you know, I'm passing up this perfect opportunity to write another erotic section.)

The key is finding one who will make you — and your finances — happy.

Date around

Financial advisor/adviser, financial planner, money coach or wealth manager? Argh. With all of their titles and trailing abbreviations, it can be so confusing to find someone you trust and who suits your needs. But the reality is that anyone (except if you're in Quebec) can call themselves a financial planner or advisor — you, my toddler, anyone. Some can sell an array of securities while others can only sell you mutual funds. Some can sell life insurance. Some are trained in tax and estate planning.

So, you need to look at their qualifications and designations to determine who you'll need. For example, if you need insurance, look for someone with an insurance licence. If you want investments in something other than mutual funds and want investment advice, look for someone registered with a securities regulator.

Start by asking your OHM tribe, your family and friends for referrals. Keep in mind that even though Uncle Ben has been handling your mom and dad's finances, he may not be the best person to manage your money and your goals. My very first financial advisor was a friend. Pro: I trusted that she was looking out for my best interests. Con: I never wanted to offend her with my money concerns or questions.

Whoever you find, google the crap out of them for reviews and make sure they're registered where they say they are. If they say they're a certified financial planner — a good designation to have — search their name online through the Financial Planning Standards Council in Canada or the CFP Board of Standards in the U.S.

This is going to be a long-term relationship, and you want to choose the right person, so plan on interviewing at least three different people. Many of my friends have admitted to me that their financial advisors cause them misery, either because they talk over their heads, ignore them or, worse, have misled or lied to them.

A good financial advisor will help you set and work toward goals, plan for bad crap and keep you accountable. A good one will check in with you regularly or meet at least once a year to discuss your progress and any new plans. A good one will be up-front about their fees and limitations. (Or the limitations of your investments — remember past performance is not an indicator of future results.)

When you find The One, don't just sit back and stare. They'll give you a questionnaire to get to know you, but get to know them and tell them what you expect to get out of this union. Take notes at meetings. Get everything in writing. Keep copies of your documents. Review your account statements.

Ask questions. Lots of questions. Pretend you're a journalist at a press conference and you need to know exactly WTF is going on so you can write a story about your money:

- Am I on track with my retirement savings?
- I want to make sure I understand. Could you explain that again, please?

- Is my portfolio properly set up and diversified to meet my goals?
- I'm sorry, what does that mean?
- What can I do to be more financially successful?
- I'm not sure I understand. Please go over that again.
- How do you respond to the leaked tape? (Nope, wait, that's for a different press conference.)

It's especially important to trust your gut and ask even more questions when something doesn't feel right. Talk to your advisor about your changing goals — which may affect your investment plan. This person should be an honorary member of your OHM tribe; they want you to succeed. Also, you pay them to do that.

It's all fun and games until someone explains mutual fund fees to you

I've run into a number of people over the years who've told me that their advisor works for free. Oh wow. How charitable! A financial fairy who sprinkles free advice in the good name of money literacy. Okay, that sarcasm sounds like Negatron's in the house, but *seriously*.

Your advisor gets paid. Maybe your bank advisor gets a salary. Maybe they're fee-based, meaning they charge you a percentage of all of the money you have invested with them. Maybe you're aware that they get their money because they're a fee-only advisor and you paid a flat fee of, say, $2,000 for a comprehensive financial plan. Or maybe they get a commission every time they buy or sell a product for you. When it comes to insurance or mutual funds, the latter is often what causes confusion.

Here's a quick and dirty lowdown on mutual fund fees.

Ongoing fees

Mutual fund fees include something called expense ratios (management expense ratio, or MER, in Canada and total expense ratio, TER, in the United States — you get it by dividing the fund costs by the fund's assets). This pays for the management of the fund and other expenses, including advertising, legal fees, stamps, staplers, etc. These so-called invisible fees are collected before returns are reported. So if the expense ratio is 2.5%, for example, and the total return is 12.5%, you'd see a return of 10%.

"Meh," you think, "if someone drank 2.5% of my coffee every morning before serving it to me, I'd never notice."

Well, if someone took 2.5% of your money every year for 30 years, you'd be pissed. Let's say we both had $5,000 to invest every year (yay us) for the next 30 years, with a rate of return of 5%.

	YOU	ME
Type of investment	Mutual fund	Exchange-traded fund (ETF)
Fund fee	2.5%	0.3%
Amount of fees paid after 30 years	$100,000	$12,000

That is a *big* difference. Oh, and my dragon is massive because what I saved in fees went to bulking up my monster.

Fees when you first buy or sell shares in a mutual fund

They're called sales loads, which sounds like a truck full of fast fashion. These fees could be a couple of percent to 10%. They fall into two types.

Front-end loads: if you invest $100,000 with a 2% front-end load, a one-time fee of $2,000 goes to the investment firm/advisor.

Back-end loads or deferred sales charges: Why is it called a back-end load? I think because you get a kick in the back end if you redeem your investment early. Essentially, you pay a fee if you sell a fund within a certain timeframe. (A typical deferred sales charge starts at about 6% of your investment in one year, declining to 0% by year seven.) If you want to avoid the ass-kicking, you have to hold onto the fund for the five to seven years, opt for "no load" funds or move the money to another fund offered by the mutual fund company.

Fund fees in Canada are among the highest in the world. (The U.S. is kicking butt in this contest.) If you want to get away from higher MER/TERs, you could always take a do-it-yourself approach with your portfolio and/or opt for ETFs and index funds, which have lower fees.

If you're okay with your mutual fund fees, at the least you should be getting good financial advice and coaching with it. The truth is, if you're starting with a small pool of money, the easiest way to access financial advice is through your bank or through a financial advisor selling mutual funds. You can always ask your advisor for lower-cost alternatives such as no-load funds (a fund without a fee when you buy or sell units) and funds without deferred sales charges (which are becoming more widespread as DSCs are becoming rarer).

If you have no idea what you're paying in mutual fund fees, look at the investment report or the fund facts or plug the name of your mutual fund into a fee calculator online. There's one at GetSmarterAboutMoney.ca and at NestWealth.com/fees.

Breaking up is hard to do

My friend Barry had a nasty break-up with his financial advisor. The advisor had put his money in mutual funds with back-end loads, even though Barry had said that he would soon want to use the money to buy a home. To get his cash out now, he'd have to incur fees of 5–6% when he sold the units. He complained to his advisor's manager and transferred his funds out of the company.

Years later, when Barry ran into the advisor, he had been let go from the firm and told Barry that he had ruined his life. "I hope you go to sleep and you think about me," he said. "I hope you die."

Ouch.

Breaking up with your financial advisor can be an emotional and stressful event — almost as traumatic as a romantic break-up. The reasons are also somewhat similar: I've found someone else (another advisor). I've changed and my needs are different (I'm done with mutual funds). I want to go out there on my own and explore my options (I'm signing up with a discount brokerage).

Your relationship with your advisor is highly charged because it is based on that all-important thing: your life savings. You've put your trust and your future in this person's hands, and when it doesn't work out, it's awkward, disappointing and potentially much worse.

Even if your advisor isn't a personal friend, money issues are sensitive and complex. You might have tried to discuss your concerns or ask questions and got a load of jargon, leaving you feeling confused, belittled or defeated.

If you're unhappy, you shouldn't spend another minute in that relationship. And you don't have to apologize for not being happy. If things are not working out, you can either just walk away and let a new advisor deal with the transition or send a Dear John letter in an email or on a Post-it note: "I'm sorry I can't don't hate me." Or better: "Thank you for your help in the past. I will be going in another direction. I will no longer be needing your services. I wish you well in your future."

Now what to do with your money? You have a few options.

You do not have to sell your investments when you fire your advisor. If the advisor has used widely available funds, you can move them "in kind" to an advisor at another investment firm or bank. You may get charged an administration fee.

However, some fund companies sell their own products and an advisor at a different company may not have access to them. If you like the products but not your advisor, opt to stay at the firm, keep your existing investments and ask a supervisor or manager to switch you to another advisor within the company.

If you want to leave the fund company, make sure you contact the firm to ask what fees you may pay if you sell your funds — remember that back-end load I was talking about. (You can look up information about the fees in the fund's prospectus.)

If the fees are too steep, you may want to leave your account as is and move the money when the deferred load/deferred sales charge (DSC) expires or gets lower; each year, often you can take out 10% of the original amount invested without being charged a DSC. Take note: your next mutual funds representative may want you to transfer your funds because they get a commission.

If you're pissed about something, there's recourse. Maybe you told your advisor that you're buying a home in six months and you need your money in a safe, low-risk investment, but they put you in a high-risk investment and your down payment is lost. Or your advisor told you that there are no fees for their service.

If a face-to-face will result in fisticuffs, put it in writing; a polite email that states the issues and your evidence will suffice. If the response is unsatisfactory, speak to the financial advisor's superior at the firm. If that doesn't settle your complaint, do a loving-kindness meditation and then contact a regulatory agency. They often investigate complaints and dole out disciplinary action, including fines and suspensions.

You'll be happier without this person in your life. You'll find someone better. And if you're feeling too burned to get into another relationship, consider learning as much as possible and DIYing your own money management. I can tell you that Barry is not thinking about his former financial advisor when he goes to sleep. Barry, and his money, are doing awesome.

YOUR HAPPY MONEY TO-DO LIST

- If you'd like some professional financial help for your happy money, ask for recommendations, look up names in your area, check their reviews and their designations.
- Interview a few. Ask what they will be delivering to you, how often they'll communicate with you and what kinds of investment products or

services they're registered to sell. Ask for references and about how they are paid.

- Make a list of questions that you have for your advisor right now. Email them!
- Set up a meeting with your advisor if you haven't done so in the last 12 months to discuss your ongoing life goals and anything that may have changed in your circumstances.
- Talk to your advisor about your mutual funds. Do you hold mutual funds with a deferred sales charge or back-end load? Ask your advisor if you hold them, and if you do, discuss why and how much it would cost you if you sold the funds today. If you have plans to sell and use the money in a year or two, then a mutual fund with a deferred load isn't the best approach.

MONEY TALKS
- If you hired a coach, what attributes would be most important to you?
- How happy are you with your advisor? What would make the relationship better?

MAKE IT RAIN

Increase your earnings and get maximum
moolah out of your life right now.

20
SHOW ME THE MONEY

I remember the day that I found out that my less experienced male colleagues were making more money than I was. I was sharing a taxi with a fellow reporter and he was ranting about how he needed a raise from his "pathetic" salary — which happened to be $10,000 higher than mine. Then he went on to talk about how much more our guy friends in the office were making.

I also remember the day that my editor told me that I would be transferred from my dream job covering arts and life and moving to financial news. My face hot, my throat tight, I blurted the terrible truth, ". . . and I never asked for a raise because I loved my job."

Yes, I can shake my fist at the systemic inequalities and the biases in our office. (Among American workers in 2015,

Black workers earned 75% as much as white workers in median hourly earnings and women earned 83% as much as men.) But I was partly responsible. I held myself back because I never asked for what I deserved. I thought my performance, my loyalty, my talent would be recognized and rewarded. I was not my best advocate. I did not fight for myself. And when you don't ask, you don't get.

It's a mistake I am trying not to repeat, but I admit it's a struggle and I continue to wrestle with it even as my career evolves. Let's make a promise to each other that we'll all do better and at least ask.

Get that raise

What you can negotiate now in terms of a pay raise could impact the rest of your life and your earning potential going forward. Understandably, many of us find asking for a raise to be stressful. While I haven't seen a study measuring the discomfort associated with salary negotiations, I'd put it up there with getting a colonoscopy or Mofo's reaction to having to drag my hair from our drains. But it doesn't have to be unpleasant and scary.

Here are five things to do before asking for a raise to make the experience easier.

1. Figure out why you deserve one. You can't march into your boss's office and demand a raise because you've been there for three years, you've been doing your job well and you heard that Susie got a raise last month. Well, you can, but you're less likely to be successful. First, you're supposed to be doing your job, so explain why you deserve more money. And ultimatums don't work with your lover and they won't with your employer. Brainstorm your accomplishments of late. Have you taken on extra responsibilities? What have you done that is above and beyond your regular duties? If it helps, put it in writing. If your boss says that they'll have to take your request to their superior, you'll have something handy to send them to back up your case.

2. Understand what your company values. You think you're doing everything that is expected of you. But have you actually checked in to ensure that you're focusing your efforts in the right place? Maybe you're super proud of the work you've done on this account; meanwhile your employer is prioritizing something else — like Susie's work. (Just kidding. I love Susie.) Plan to request a raise in the future; right now, go send an email to your boss requesting a meeting where you can talk about your goals ("What does success look like a year from now in this role?").

3. Do your homework. Knowing when to approach your employer is important, whether it be during your performance review or before your company's new fiscal year begins. Also, know how much you want. Check job sites such as GlassDoor.com and Monster.ca for positions and wages, as well as government and local sites. Survey people in similar positions at other companies. Figure out the pay scales within your own company. Human resources consulting companies report that the average pay raise has fallen between 2% and 3% in the last few years. Workers in the oil and gas industry will see the highest salary increases while those in pharmaceutical, biotech, wholesale and retail will see the smallest. Propose a range to make you appear more flexible. Negotiation expert Fotini Iconomopoulos says it can be important to throw out the first number because of anchoring bias — our tendency to fixate on the first number put forth in a negotiation (the anchor) and to use that as a starting point. Aim high.

4. Rehearse your points. Plan for contingencies. (What will you say if they say "no" or if they offer you less than you want?) Don't be afraid to pause and reflect before you speak. Don't be afraid to extend your pause if you need 24 hours to think over any offers. And relax and try to smile during your meeting. Your success is not determined by a staring contest with your boss.

5. Determine what demands are most important to you and bring them all to the table during your meeting. You don't always have to negotiate for money. Your company may be willing to fork over something else in lieu of a pay raise: free parking, additional vacation, more or less travel, opportunities to work on high-profile projects, etc.

What should you say in salary negotiations? Here are some sample scripts. (Tip: Don't be Negatron. Be Optimist Prime.)

> Bosslady: What do you want to talk about today?
> Negatron: Show me the money!
> Optimist Prime: I asked for this meeting to talk about my compensation. I've been reflecting on the things that I've been doing over the past year. I've brought on two new clients who are contributing 15% of the organization's current revenue. Every quarter, I was able to negotiate having our logo on these Super Fabulous Places. My salary has been on the same level since I started this position in

March 2015, and my contributions to this company show that I've earned the raise that I am requesting.

Bosslady: How much were you making at your last job? (In a growing number of places, it's illegal to ask about salary history.)

Negatron: Oh, lots.

Optimist Prime: I'd like to keep the focus on this role. Based on research and the requirements for this position, I'm looking for a range of $45,000 to $55,000.

Bosslady: Well, we're tightening our belts right now and don't have the money in the budget.

Negatron: If you have money for Susie, you have money for me. If you have money to put a new fridge in the staff room, then you have money for me.

Optimist Prime: I appreciate that the company has financial constraints. However, investing in my ability to continue being successful and continue making this organization successful is worth discussing.

Bosslady: I get what you're saying, but I'll have to take your request to the higher-ups.

Negatron: Can I talk to them directly?

Optimist Prime: How can I help you take my request forward? May I put my accomplishments in writing for you?

Bosslady: Sounds good. How much are you looking for?

Negatron: How much do you have?

Optimist Prime: I've researched salaries and to be competitive with others in our industry, the range tends to be around $50,000 to $55,000. I'm making $48,000 and given what I've demonstrated in the past year, I'd appreciate between $52,000 and $55,000.

Bosslady: No. We can't do it right now.

Negatron: [*Arm sweeps all of the papers and frames off her desk.*]

Optimist Prime: Thank you for your time. I enjoy working for this company and I value my colleagues. While I value these things, I also want to be compensated and recognized for the contributions I make to the organization. I'd like to understand what I need to do to create a greater opportunity to increase my pay when the financial state is better. I want to ensure that I'm focusing my efforts in the right place.

When it comes to getting more money from your employer, you could sit at your cubicle with a sign that says, "Will work for a raise." You could passively aggressively moan about how expensive childcare is at every staff meeting. Or you could meet with your boss to tell them (honestly) how much you've been kicking ass and how much value you're adding to the company. Be brave enough to ask. The answer could be yes.

YOUR HAPPY MONEY TO-DO LIST

- Thinking of asking for a raise? Research what you are worth. Find out what your position pays but get the facts regarding your education, certifications, skills, ability and experience as well as location. Check job sites for positions and wages, and survey people in similar positions at other companies. Figure out the pay scales within your own company.
- When you are speaking with your boss, don't wing it. I run scenarios with my besties beforehand. (It gives them the opportunity to practise different voices and to give me a hard time.)

MONEY TALKS

- Are you a good negotiator? What qualities make for a great negotiator?
- In what ways do you excel at your job?
- How do you go above and beyond in your job?

21
HAPPY HUSTLING

If Mofo were a rapper, his name would be Sir Spend-A-Lot, and the lyrics to his famed song would be "I like big bucks and I cannot lie."

For all of the ribbing and nicknames, Mofo is good at making money. When he was a boy, he set up shop in his basement and sold sports cards to the neighbourhood kids. When he was a teenager, he employed a student to make fake IDs to sell around school. He was selling things on the internet when there was a screech and ring to connect to it. He grew up fantasizing about mansions and sports cars and having an executive office with a shower in it.

I never grew up wanting to be rich. I wanted to pursue my passion. This works perfectly as a quote on a mug but not so much as a motivator to make cash. It didn't help that on my first day of journalism school, the professor told us, "If you want to be rich, there's the door." I thought, "Whatever, I'm going to be embedded as a war correspondent, subsisting off instant noodles (which I love)." (Oh, 18-year-old Melissa was so cute.)

I've always been inclined to cut back on spending rather than seek ways to make more money. Mofo opened my eyes. As an entrepreneur from a family of self-made men and women, he's always on the lookout for opportunities, and he always stresses getting what you're worth. He told me that it didn't matter how many damn coupons I clipped, I'd never be wealthy without making more money. I told him that it didn't matter how much money he brought in if he didn't know how to save it and invest it.

We're both right.

We need money for our life, our family and our goals, and I've talked about how to be smarter and happier with what we have. There are only so many expenses that we can cut (how many times can a person reuse dental floss?), but there is no limit to how much more money you can make.

While, absolutely, we can make more cash to give ourselves more opportunities, we have to remind ourselves that once we have more — more for panty closets and candy walls and heated toilet seats or whatever — it won't do much for our self-worth and our innate happiness.

Do the hustle

Today, it's never been easier to make more money if you have the willingness, time and determination. The side hustle has become increasing popular with the ease of e-commerce and with the rise of the on-demand gig economy; you can do everything from selling your sock puppets on Etsy to walking dogs in your free time. Forty-four million Americans have a side hustle, says a 2017 Bankrate study. And of those who are earning extra money on the side, 36% are making $500 or more per month. That's not small change.

You want to save more for a house down payment and have your latte and drink it too? You want to be debt-free by the end of the year? Start your own thing.

I've had a lot of side hustles over the years. And I've run in circles where everyone is a "slash" (architect/drummer, teacher/restaurant hostess, wealth advisor/fitness trainer). My side hustles were all passion projects and excuses to hang with friends. Work was always fun, which reduced the risk of burnout. Venture capitalist and the youngest member of the *Dragons' Den*, Michele Romanow, often talks about making her fun cost-neutral. So, think about what you enjoy doing and how you can make money — whether that's live-streaming your video games or teaching Zumba or selling your photographs to a stock agency.

You also have to find work that fits into your schedule. Maybe you're making food deliveries in the evening or knitting while the baby sleeps and selling your booties online. But more jobs obviously mean more working hours. More than 40% of multiple job holders reported to Statistics Canada that they worked more than 50 hours a week. You have to consider whether those sideline hours are the best use of your time.

If you start to burn out, check if your work is fulfilling a specific goal. For example, if the side job is to help pay down your debt, commit to doing it for a set period of time or until you hit a certain credit card balance. If you feel exhausted, take a break for self-care. (I'm talking to you, moms.)

Approach your moonlighting gig like you would a carefully planned meal. You wouldn't want to ruin your boeuf bourguignon by scattering Cheetos onto the plate as a side. Ideally, your side job should have a purpose other than offering extra cash, such as beefing up your resumé or providing benefits (Starbucks and Costco offer benefits to part-timers, for example).

You don't want your full-time job to suffer. Also, make sure that your multiple jobs don't put you in awkward positions with your employer, co-workers, clients or customers. (It might be weird if you walked into a room for a massage and found the practitioner was your accountant.) Your side gig should not put you in a conflict of interest with your main job nor put that full-time job, or your well-being, at risk.

Take your side money seriously. Earmark those earnings for your priorities and put them in a separate account or automate your savings. Don't just spend it or get used to spending it; you don't want your side gig to have to be a permanent gig because you grow used to higher lifestyle expenses.

Fortunately, people who freelance or run their own business can take advantage of deductions to reduce their taxable income. For example, if you spend $2,000 on materials and equipment to get your online sock puppet shop going, and you make $5,000 that year, you can deduct the $2,000 as business expenses and only pay taxes on $3,000. Track your income and keep a record of all of your expenses. Opening a separate bank account and credit card for your business may help you to be better organized. Some of my moonlighting colleagues use the FreshBooks app — bookkeeping software for small businesses that, for a monthly fee, sends invoices and tracks time and expenses.

HOW TO FIND A PASSION PROJECT

What are you passionate about? I'm passionate about chips, but unless I get into webcam eating or land a rare food-tasting gig, I likely won't make a lot of money from my love of nachos. How does one find a project or job that is enjoyable and intrinsically motivating? Here are four questions to help.

1. What makes you forget to eat, put off peeing and skip sleep? Do you remember a time when you were so engrossed in an activity that everything else came second, even fundamental bodily needs?
2. What did you love to do as a kid? What gave you joy — long before you had to worry about bills, a regular paycheque or building a career?
3. What would you do for free? If money was no object, what would you do with your time? (The truth is that your venture might not make any money in the beginning so, essentially, you may end up working for free for a bit.)
4. What would you be willing to fail at? No successful venture comes without failures or mistakes. You have to be okay looking like an ass at something for a while.

Take on something new

After I wrote my first teen vampire novel in 2010, I pitched about 20 literary agents but no one bit. In a post-*Twilight* world, vampire queries made agents recoil in horror. One agent tweeted that she'd die if she got any more vampire pitches.

So, I mustered the courage to publish it myself under the pen name Wynne Channing (it's my stripper name: my middle name and the street I grew up on). I wasn't sure how much money to invest in it — you could spend a few hundred to thousands. "What is your dream worth?" a friend asked. Good point, I said, but with that attitude, I'd soon be in debt, selling sentences on the street. ("Will write for food. Give me your two cents and I'll throw in a pun.")

I paid an editor about $2,000 to edit my manuscript. I found an artist online who designed my book cover for $400. I spent $150 on formatting my e-book. I paid a PR company $375 to organize a blog tour. But my biggest investment was time. I knew nothing about self-publishing or marketing. And there was a lot to learn and do.

While working full-time and dancing three days a week, I ran my own publishing company in the wee hours. I kept the hours of, well, a vampire, and the sleep deprivation turned my sharp and efficient brain into mush. For example, one day at the newspaper where I worked, I got an email to interview "the president of Ups." I called and told him in a voicemail how happy I would be to chat about "Ups" — as in "up" and "down." The moment I put the receiver down, I froze. Oh. My. God. UPS Shipping.

That night, I went to bed early. But for a month after, my friends called me "Ups."

I was in New York interviewing Alexander Skarsgård,

who then played a vampire on the show *True Blood*, when I saw my first review for my book. "I could not put it down," the U.K. reader wrote. The book series has thousands of reviews now. It hit number one on a number of Amazon's bestseller lists and at one point ranked 221 out of more than a million books in the Kindle store.

I didn't get rich, however, off paranormal fiction, but it's been years since I published the books and, with no ongoing promotion, I'll still get a random royalties cheque in the mail. The residual income can add up to a few thousand dollars a year.

But the true value was the experience. It was a great adventure, and I learned so much — knowledge and skills that have helped with my other work. The process also boosted my confidence and expanded my self-definition. Experiences can make us happy, and your side hustle could be the ultimate experience.

I'm not afraid of tackling things that I don't know anything about — that's the nature of my work as a reporter. You start the day with nothing and by the end of it, you could have written 1,000 informed words on anything from the latest trends in cancer treatments to the inner workings of a plane when it is struck by lightning. If you don't know something, you go and find out. You're constantly chasing what you don't know.

When was the last time that you were presented with an opportunity to try something new? What's something that you've always wanted to learn about or do? If you're turning something down because you're "not good at it" or you "know nothing about it," then you're cutting off any opportunity to learn or get better at it. You're blocking your own growth. And to grow is to be happy.

Be the CEO

Mofo is the president and CEO of his own company: because he works from home, he finally has a shower in his office. He just has to share the shower with another president and CEO. Me. Since leaving my newspaper job and using the skills I learned being an authorpreneur, I built a new career under my own name.

In the confines of our office where nine-to-fivers can't hate on us, Mofo and I will say to each other, "TGI-don't know what day it is!" Because every day could be a weekend. On the flip side, every day could be a work day. And when you work for yourself, every day *is* a work day; every day is a day where you are responsible for putting in the time and effort or you don't get paid.

But when the pay finally comes, you have the potential to make more money than you ever thought possible. CEO-level money. Many of my loved ones have launched their own businesses and with mad hustle, good ideas (often recycled from crappy ideas) and some luck, they've created successful, lucrative ventures.

Before you go into business with your own damn self, consider these three things.

1. Are you a self-starter? Your new boss (you) will have to crack the whip.
2. Can you problem-solve to get through setbacks? If you look at problems as solutions waiting to happen, you're in the right line of work.
3. Can you stand financial instability and living on less? It could take a while for your business to be profitable, and the launch often takes a lot of capital and resources. Be prepared for this.

Many of us, including Mofo and me, have started a thing, put a thing out into the world and had it fail. Mofo's had several businesses over the years, and I've seen him through the promise and excitement of the beginning and the frustration and heartbreak of roadblocks. The years have been punctuated by brainstorming sessions, lists of awful company and product names, 3 a.m. phone calls with suppliers in other timezones and heated negotiations with partners or freelancers. In his mid-20s, he once ordered a supply of blue car headlights from overseas; they came haphazardly sprayed with blue paint. What do you do with hundreds of unsellable light bulbs? And how do you complain to a supplier who doesn't speak your language? Once, he created a product, paid for a logo, built a website and started selling, only to have another company tell him that they had the exclusive rights to his company name.

You troubleshoot, pivot, fail, try again and troubleshoot. Every blip was a lesson to help us in the next adventure. You just have to risk failing. There could be something on the other side of your fear that will be so damn great. You just have to start and then have the tenacity to stick with it. Giving up midway would be like turning the heat off just before the water boils.

THREE STARTER QUESTIONS TO TEST YOUR IDEA, SERVICE OR PRODUCT

1. What problem are you solving with your business?
2. What's the competition doing? And what secret ingredient is in your special sauce?

> 3. How much money/resources/time do you
>   need to put in to get this off the ground
>   (and how much do you have)?

The skills to pay the bills

You determine your worth by every single job that you take or piece that you produce — Mofo's always drilling this into me. When I started working for myself, I felt the pressure of having no income. Like a starving animal, I wanted to jump at every opportunity thrown at me.

I was also met with a barrage of empowering messages about my worth. Know your worth and then add tax. Charge people what you deserve. Don't work for free. Have confidence. (Okay, Instagram meme. No problem.)

I've never been one to rest on my laurels. For me, success is a privilege to be earned. I could fake it until I made it, but to truly feel confident, I have to grow it organically. That's what has pushed me to bring my A-game to every single project whether it is free or not. So in the beginning, I did work that did not necessarily pay a lot to gain experience, to workshop my presentations, to test my product, to get reviews, endorsements and content for my website. I looked at what others were charging for similar services, and I spoke to many people in the same field to ask for advice on what to charge. I got a range and I decided where I fell.

Even still, I was screwing myself.

I once quoted what I thought was a really, really, really, ridiculously high price for my services. I ended up passing the job to a colleague who took my quote and doubled it.

I've learned and moved on (after my inner voice moaned like a crowd seeing a dude get hit in the nads).

I forgot that I'm a sum of so many parts. When someone hires me, they're not getting someone who has been in business for a year, they're getting someone with decades of experience. Don't sell yourself short; you have many skills that you bring to the table. And don't make sacrifices if they are not in line with your values.

I only work three days a week. I work in a frenzy during those three days — it's the kind of day where I'm having phone meetings while driving to other meetings. But the rest of the week is for family, for friends, for sandcastles and couch forts (for grocery store tantrums and gooey pink eye, let's be real, parentals). For more snuggles and squeals and less screens and scrolling. I say "no" a lot — to my toddler, to opportunities. But as boss, I must set standards and boundaries to protect my happiness.

As a freelancer, as an entrepreneur, you show the world what you're worth. The same goes for anyone negotiating a salary. Show them what you aspire to be, not what your self-conscious, hesitant self whispers to you.

YOUR HAPPY MONEY TO-DO LIST

- What could your side hustle be? Make a list of all the work that you could do; look for work in your field, like consulting, and for work that will enhance your skills. Brainstorm with your OHM tribe and ask trusted people for suggestions of what you could be good at.
- If you dream of starting your own business, connect with other entrepreneurs and talk to them about their experiences. Know a stay-at-home

mom who sells lipstick? Buy a Ravishing Red from her and pick her brain. If you are self-employed, reach out to as many people in your field as possible and look for mentors.

- Spend a few minutes getting familiar with an online platform where you can sell your goods or services, such as Etsy or Fiverr or Upwork.
- For those who are self-employed or have a side hustle, to make tax time more endurable, consider making a date with another self-employed friend to tally up your receipts. Self-employment can be lonely. Connect with others.
- Look into apps that will make your accounting easier (FreshBooks) or help you file receipts (Receipts by Wave).

MONEY TALKS

- If you could do anything for a living, what would you do?
- What do you find most fulfilling about the work that you are currently doing? What would make the work day better or more productive?
- If you've ever started a business that didn't take off or had a side gig that went sour, what did you learn?

22
COUCH CUSHION CASH

While I've learned to be more entrepreneurial over the years, I've always been cheap. Who doesn't enjoy making a few bucks with minimal effort or brain power? I've taken paintings out of a hotel dumpster and resold them on Kijiji. I've shared my thoughts about products in front of a one-way glass in exchange for $50 to $100. I've collected bottles of booze left at the curb to return for spare change.

Sometimes salary negotiations are on hold. Sometimes the idea of a regular side hustle is just too much to process. And sometimes, it's just nice to get a few extra bucks here and there. Well, you can still make extra cash in your own way. Without dumpster diving, I promise.

From crap to cash

Mofo treats his electronics as if he's borrowed them from an extremely anal friend. He carefully handles them, cleans them and hoards the packaging because he knows that he'll eventually sell it on eBay with the abbreviation EUC (excellent used condition).

I'm terrible with my electronics; as soon as I get them, my phones just dive out of my hand toward pavement. (Mofo's started covering my phones in tactical gear.) But if something I no longer use is in good condition, I usually find it a new home; it makes me feel happy to know someone else will derive joy from something I no longer do.

My friends and I read Marie Kondo's *The Life-Changing Magic of Tidying Up*, where she instructs you to go through your possessions and ask yourself if the item sparks joy. Whatever we deemed un-joyful, we donated or sold. Whether through Craigslist, Kijiji, eBay, online apps, Facebook's Marketplace, a garage sale or your local consignment store, you can easily unload your unwanted items for extra cash. According to a report by Kijiji, second-hand sellers netted $1,134 on average in 2017.

My bestie makes that and more every year selling her stuff. Numbers are scribbled all over a shoe box in her room; the latest number reads $1,600 — the amount of money she made on a Facebook auction page in one summer. I've unloaded a third of my wardrobe on my local Facebook "bidding wars" group. The items are up for auction for 24 hours and pick up must be done within 48 hours of winning. I mostly do porch pickups, where I'll hang the item on my mailbox and the buyer leaves the money under my welcome mat (I've never been ripped off).

If you're going to sell something online, don't just throw it up there without thought or strategy. Maximize your second-hand sale with these five quick tips.

1. Timing is important. If you have a winter coat to sell, wait until patio season is over.
2. Do your research and see what an item similar to yours is selling for second-hand.
3. Provide all the details in the post — condition, dimensions, size, etc. — and use a detailed and catchy headline ("Brand new treadmill for sale because I'm lazy"). Humour generates more views on ads, Kijiji says.
4. Always use a photo — a good-quality photo that shows the item in focus and under proper lighting.
5. And if you get inquiries, respond promptly. People lose interest quickly.
6. If you're getting rid of something, take a moment to consider why you're parting with it and let that inform your buying habits going forward.

EIGHT WAYS TO MAKE EXTRA MONEY

Need more cash? Try one of these tactics to make some extra dough.

1. Rent your place on Airbnb while you're on vacation (if you own your house/condo and your condo board is cool with it).

2. Sign up to take part in paid focus groups. (One of my friends participated in a focus group where she had to taste chocolate. Tough work.)

3. Rent your car with an online service such as Turo.

4. Get gift cards and money for odd jobs such as surfing the web or taking polls or watching videos, using Swagbucks or InboxDollars. (Disclaimer: Make sure you research the online company or service that is offering work. Never pay to sign up or share your financial information. Watch out for scams such as fraudsters asking you to be a mystery shopper and sending you a cheque to cash. A legitimate employer will never send you funds then ask for a portion back.)

5. Do paid online surveys.

6. Sell your photos from your smartphone through apps such as FOAP or Twenty20.

7. Sell your hair. If your hair is longer than six inches, you can sell it at HairSellOn.com.

8. Think like an entrepreneurial teen and offer your manpower to the neighbourhood. Walk dogs. Mow lawns. Offer to babysit; your neighbours (people like me) will be happy to get out and fraternize with other adults, maybe see an R-rated film and eat at a restaurant without a children's menu.

I'd like to remind you, however, to put a value on your time. If it takes you an hour to do a paid survey for a few bucks, is that a worthwhile use of your time? If you're doing it while watching TV, maybe. My bestie spends a lot of time preparing and monitoring her online sales; however, she thinks the whole process is fun.

YOUR HAPPY MONEY TO-DO LIST

- Do a regular inventory of your home and collect things that will fetch a decent return. Organize a summer everything-must-go yard sale with your OHM tribe to declutter and donate anything that doesn't get purchased. Ask your best friend to come over and help you clean out your closet *Queer Eye* style.
- Brainstorm ways that you can earn some extra bucks.

MONEY TALKS

- How much money would you accept to do tedious things that you don't enjoy? Assign a minimum dollar figure per hour to do the following: shovelling snow, transcribing a conversation, reading company newsletters.
- How do you know when you're ready to let go of things you own?

HAPPINESS ASSASSINS

Being happy isn't all about adding positives;
for better results, nix negatives
wherever possible.

23
DEBT: THE BIG KILLJOY

When it comes to money and happiness, there is no lesson that I can impart that will be more important than this one: the biggest happiness killer is debt. The Life Events Inventory, a 2001 U.K. study, ranked 56 of life's most stressful experiences. Where do you think "getting into debt beyond means of repayment" ranked?

Problems with your boss ranked #36. Your spouse cheating on you was #14. The death of a close friend, #13; divorce, #9; a period of homelessness, #6.

Getting into debt ranked #5.

Debt is one of the biggest predictors of relationship strife. Every 10-fold increase in consumer debt is associated with a 7% increase in the likelihood of divorce, according to research out of Utah State University. High debt is associated with health issues, including higher blood pressure and mental health problems.

To be happy, you must tackle that sucker. You can do it. I've interviewed many people over the years who have been able to dig themselves out of ginormous holes. These were people who were languishing on debt row. They had maxed out their credit cards. They were stuck deciding which bill to pay each month and only making minimum payments. They were raiding their retirement funds to cover bills. One 48-year-old father of three had racked up $85,000 in consumer debt. At one time, he had to flick through his credit cards, as if he was going through a half pack of playing cards. He sought help, buckled down and now only has one credit card with a $300 limit. Another young man I spoke to racked up a $20,000 balance by the time he was 23; after maxing out one $15,000 card, the company increased his limit to $45,000. He reined in his spending, got a second job and put more than $500 every month into his accounts until he was debt-free four years later.

If you're drowning in an undertow of debt, I don't want you to feel like an ass. Or a lost cause. You're not alone. Surveys have shown that almost half of us carry credit card debt. We have a lot of credit options — credit cards, leasing companies, private lenders — and people are offering it to you everywhere you go. Last week, I was in a grocery store and near the deli section, a woman offered me a credit card like she was offering me a ham sampler. We've been able to borrow more with historically low interest rates, and we can shuffle our debt by transferring loans to new credit suppliers.

Getting in debt has become so easy that we're numb to it. If you had told previous generations that they should take out a line of credit to pay for a vacation, your parents/grandparents would slap you upside the head (because in previous generations, parents punished with spankings while we change wifi passwords).

Once you have the ability to charge it, spending is all too seductive. Merchants and retailers are trying to make buying as easy as snapping your fingers; in the retail/banking industry, they call these "frictionless" transactions, which sounds like they're talking about the condom market. Credit cards anesthetize the pain of spending. So now you just tap your money away, buy with one click or rely on auto-renewals.

With what we're up against, absolutely it can be a struggle. The Happy Go Money journey is personal and it can be a long one, with hits and misses. But you're a fighter. Your mistakes, your bad choices, your losses: they don't define who you are today.

And I hear you saying, "Melissa, this isn't making me very happy right now." It will. I promise. You have to look at the big picture. Hey, no one likes going to the dentist, but having teeth will make you plenty happy in the end.

Fight debt

When you're battling debt, start by listing your opponents: credit card balances, lines of credit, mortgages, unsecured loans, automobile financing, student debts, pay advances, outstanding bills, loans from family and friends and so on. If you can, include their corresponding interest rates. With the interest rate handy, plug the numbers into a free online debt repayment calculator; adjust how much you think you can put against that debt every month and see how long it'll take you to eliminate it.

We need to prioritize which to tackle first. If you owe money to the taxman and they're calling you, don't ignore them. They're charging you compound daily interest on what you owe. They have incredible powers to collect money owed to them, including garnishing your wages, seizing your assets (including your house), closing your business and freezing your bank accounts.

That Darth Vader–level foe aside, facing your biggest debt can be discouraging — it could feel like you're bouncing off a sumo wrestler. I get that the little guys are easier to pick off. And it feels good to do so, building confidence and motivation after each victory. Personal finance is, well, personal so you should do whatever charges you up. But if you're a smart fighter, you'll overlook the little guys to first deal with the debt that is causing you to bleed the most — the debt with the highest interest rate.

For many of us, this is our credit card debt.

Get drastic on your plastic

When I was in university, the banks set up booths on campus peddling credit cards. "As a bonus, get a free hat!" the reps said. My father had given me the "with power comes great responsibility" lecture when it came to credit cards, but many of my peers signed up. I wanted to tell them to hang onto their hats when the credit card bills came. I've spoken to tons of people who got themselves in trouble with their first credit cards. No one explained to them how interest rates worked, what minimum payments meant and how their credit could be destroyed.

For example, let's say you use your credit card to buy a $2,000 patio set. Your card has an 18% APR (annual percentage rate, or interest rate). If you only made the minimum payment of 2% or $10 a month (whichever is higher), you'd spend more than 30 years paying off the set. I don't even know if my teeth will last that long, let alone a wicker chaise longue, and I definitely don't want Silver Fox to be still paying for anything that I buy today (including my house). On top of the $2,000 price tag, through the wonder — or in this case, horror — of compounding interest, you'll have paid more than $4,900 in interest. There's that dragon that I was talking about earlier, but this one's playing for the other team — you've gone from being the Mother of Dragons to dragon food.

But if you put $150 a month against your debt (and assuming you don't buy any more outdoor decor), you'd be square in a year and three months and drop almost $250 to interest payments. Better. Not the best. But better.

If you always pay off your credit card balance in full every month, then carry on. But if you have a balance that you want to wipe out, take that credit card out of your wallet. Delete your credit card information from your computer browser. Whenever someone says they're trying to get rid of debt and I see them swipe their credit card, I think of *The Simpsons* episode where the townsfolk have literally dug themselves into a deep hole: "How are we going to get out of here?" Otto asks. "We'll dig our way out!" Homer exclaims. Then Chief Wiggum retorts, "No, dig up, stupid!"

I have friends who, rather than dig, bury their heads in the sand and do nothing. You can try to ignore it, but like the weeds in your yard or your mother-in-law, it'll just become more powerful. Do something. Do anything to pay down your balance. To anyone starting the hard work of confronting credit card debt, my hat's off to you.

QUIZ: SCORE YOUR
CREDIT SCORE KNOW-HOW

Your credit score is a number grading you on your behaviour with debt. My inner 12-year-old is ready to explode hearing this ("I need an A+!!!"), clearly why I was so popular in school. (My scholastic obsessions plus my dental head gear made me wicked cool.)

The scores range from 300 to 900. Anything under 650 kind of sucks. Basically, if you ever need to borrow money, a low score means you won't be getting the best offers (the lowest mortgage rates, for example). You should check your credit score and credit report at least once a year to make sure it's accurate — and to assess your finances.

It's quiz time! (My inner student just fainted.) Do you know what it takes to have a good credit score? Answer true or false to each statement.

1. You have a bunch of credit cards, but you only use one. Closing your unused credit card accounts will help improve your credit score.
2. You max out your credit cards. But you always pay them off in full so it shouldn't affect your credit score.
3. Sometimes, you'll skip a monthly credit card payment because as long as the balance is less than $10, it doesn't hurt your score.

4. In terms of your credit score, having a car loan, a credit card and a mortgage is a better debt mix than having five credit cards.
5. Applying for a new cellphone account could count as a hit to your credit score.

Now let's see how you did.

1. FALSE. Closing accounts can actually hurt your score. You could be closing an old account that is shoring up your score. History makes up 15% of your score. The longer you have an account open, the better.
2. FALSE. Credit usage accounts for 30% of your score. If your debt is at capacity all the time, it doesn't bode well for your score. Set an imaginary limit on your credit cards of 70%; for example, if your limit is $1,000, try not to borrow more than $700.
3. FALSE. Never, never miss a payment, even if it's a few dollars. At the least, make the minimum payment. About 35% of your credit score is based on your payment history.
4. TRUE. All debts aren't created equal. Your credit mix makes up 10% of your score. There are two kinds of credit. The first is revolving credit such as credit cards and lines of credit. You pay them down and the credit becomes available again. The second

is instalment credit — personal loans
repaid with fixed scheduled payments,
such as a student or car loan or a mortgage. It's good to have a mix of the two.

5. TRUE. Credit inquiries make up 10% of
your overall credit score. New accounts
and credit checks can affect your credit
score, so getting a car loan or signing
up for a cellphone plan can negatively
impact your score. Free online credit
checks through places such as Borrowell,
Mogo and RateHub are considered soft
checks and don't affect your score. Also,
multiple credit checks when you're shopping for a car or mortgage loan are often
counted as one.

Keep punching

Okay, if this were a video game, every boss that you beat
would give you more munition to fight the next.

Look at your spending plan. Where can you get extra
dollars to put to your debt? Can you cut back somewhere
or pick up some extra shifts at work? Can you automate a
monthly payment? Make the minimum payment on all of
your debts and throw all of your extra punches at the loan
with the highest interest rate.

Once that is cleared, you're going to roll the money you
were paying on that debt into the next balance. With the
momentum and with the extra money freed up from not

having to pay interest on those other debts, every subsequent punch will be that much bigger and stronger.

What about your other pools of money? Silver Fox is saying, "Don't you dare touch my money." I'm not talking about your retirement funds. But do you have a bunch of money in a high interest savings account that isn't invested in anything? I know that is for emergencies and that is super important. But this may be more pressing. Keep a little, just in case, and try to stop the bleed before it becomes a *financial* emergency.

What about your spouse's pool? I know couples where one person has a stash of cash and the other has high interest debt. But the debt is his fault so he has to deal with it, she says. Okay, I am not Dr. Phil. I'm not getting into a couples counselling session with anyone, but you're a team. Try to have a conversation (maybe after a nice dinner or during a leisurely walk) about whether a bailout makes sense if the person is willing to take responsibility and change their ways — maybe they agree to start putting money aside for a shared goal, for example. It's better to owe your spouse a year's worth of back rubs than to owe massive amounts of money on your credit card.

Debt consolidation and transfers
(or different pile, same shit)

Let's talk about this because digging a hole to fill another hole comes with risks. If I had debts on three credit cards (with interest rates at 18%, 22% and 29%), I might be able to get a loan from a bank to cover those balances. Then I'd only owe the bank at a much lower interest rate with monthly instalments. That's what we call consolidation.

The way to get the cheapest interest rates would be to

have your bank lend you money against the equity in your home; this comes in the form of a home equity line of credit or a refinancing of your home or a second mortgage. You can also use your line of credit or apply to see if you're eligible for one. Remember though, home equity loans and secured lines of credit use your assets as collateral. A credit card company can only harass you for cash and crap on your credit score, but they can't confiscate your house.

You need to get real and fix the behaviour that led to the debt in the first place — otherwise, you'll end up in a deeper hole. One of my good friends refused to use her line of credit to pay off her $9,000 credit card debt because she knew the problem wasn't the interest rate. *She* was the problem. She needed to address her behaviour before she added to her misery with more pools of debt. Just because you've consolidated your debts, doesn't mean you can get lazy, sit back and chill.

Another strategy to consider is transferring your credit card debt from a high interest card to one with a lower interest rate. You'll often see credit cards offering free transfers with maybe six or 12 months of zero- or low-interest rates. If you take this route, keep these five important things in mind.

1. First, look out for transfer fees.
2. Find out what the low rates apply to — some don't cover new charges. If you're using the new card as a strategy to punch debt, transfer your balance, throw money at it and don't make any new purchases on it.
3. How long does this low-interest period last? Make sure you pay down the debt within the

low-interest period because sometimes rates can rise higher than what you were paying before.

4. Don't miss a payment. The lender could cut off its promotional rate in retaliation.

5. Shop around. If you get a quote for a lower rate from another company, tell your existing company that you're considering a balance transfer. They could come to the table and help you out. This is a good practice in general, especially if you don't end up transferring or consolidating your debt and continue to carry that balance.

Seriously. Call your credit card company now and, in your firm but polite voice, ask for a lower interest rate. Tell them that you've been loyal for X number of years and another company has been looking your way, offering you a better deal. Tell them that you feel unappreciated, and that you gave them the best years of your life — okay, maybe we're confusing our feelings with something else — but ask them to match the other company's rate or at least lower theirs. I'm unbending with customer service agents. The moment I hear a slight unhelpful tone in their voice, a pause, an "unfortu—" I thank them, hang up and call back to get another person. I almost always ask for the supervisor. And I almost always get something for my troubles, for my loyalty, for my concerns. (Twice this week, I hung up and called back for a more helpful customer service agent at my bank and at my gas company, and both times, the second person said, "No problem. I'll help.")

Finally, you can work with a reputable non-profit credit counselling organization to consolidate your debts into one monthly payment. The service also comes with education to help you set good money habits. But make sure you research the organization. Read their reviews online and check with the Better Business Bureau and local consumer protection agencies. Check to see if they are appropriately licensed and if their counsellors are certified. Be wary of any high fees and read the fine print. Any service claiming to be a debt doctor with the ability to erase your negative credit reports to repair your credit is bullshit. The only way to get out of debt and to fix your credit score is to do the work and pay your bills on time.

Debt traps

When you're fighting debt, things can get dirty. Watch out for these low blows.

The no-money down: When you sign up for one of those "no interest and no money down" financing deals, there are some things to consider. Note that when purchasing in the store, there could be administrative fees of around $100 at the time of purchase. I know we're excited that we're getting the couch immediately, but stop and find out: is the interest waived or deferred? If the interest is deferred, it could mean that if you don't pay it off in full before the deadline — even if you only have a few dollars left one day after the deadline — you'll pay all of the interest you would have paid that year, and at a rate as high as 30%. If you opt for this, know when the deadline is and set a reminder at least a month prior. You need to give yourself ample time for the payment to clear and to be forwarded to the correct finance company. And don't miss a payment. If you're late paying, you could be charged interest on the outstanding balance or billed for all of the interest accrued since making the purchase. Ouch.

Cash advances: When you get a cash advance on your credit card, you start accruing interest the minute you take out the money (unlike with a credit card purchase where you have a grace period). Almost every credit card will charge you an upfront cash-advance fee in the form of a percentage of your transaction or a flat fee of say $3.50. You're also likely dealing with higher interest rates than with everyday purchases. Those cheques that the credit card companies send you in the mail? Those are considered cash advances if you use them.

Pay-day loans: Pay-day loan providers seem to be everywhere, and now they're online. "Borrow $100–$1,000 fast," explains one mobile app. "Easy 2-minute form. Instant results. Cash wired directly to your bank. Bad credit OK." No. Not okay. People can expect to pay up to 25% interest — even if they repay the loan in a few days. If you take out $1,000, you have to pay back $1,250. This kind of interest will kill you.

Good debt

Good debt, to me, sounds like an oxymoron, like jumbo shrimp or Biggie Smalls. So-called good debt is when you borrow money to buy something that will grow in value or pay off in the long term — taking out a student loan to pay for a college education, getting a mortgage for a home or rental property or taking out a business loan to buy equipment for your start-up. "See?" you might say. "Not all debt is villainous." But I think all debt has the potential to be evil. Remember Darth Vader started out as a pudgy-faced, pod-racing Anakin Skywalker.

Here are some examples of how good debt can go bad.

- You take out a massive student loan to get a degree in mythology and folklore, but you have no intention of using it to find work — and there's little work in this field for you.
- You spend a big portion of your student loan on clothes, travel and other non-school-related things.
- You buy the maximum-valued house that the bank qualifies you for, but the monthly costs to carry the mortgage prevent you from saving for other things.
- You buy the maximum-valued house that the bank qualifies you for, but you'll be paying for it until you're 71. (Silver Fox is pissed.)

We all need to be warier of debt, even the kind that starts out as good. Sometimes we let our emotions, our greed or our ambitions draw us more into debt because we think the reward will be great. But sometimes it isn't what's best for our happiness or our finances.

Another example is when people tell me that they're borrowing money to buy stocks or trade currency on the foreign exchange market. Listen, I'm not against the idea of borrowing to invest in an asset, which is called leveraging in the finance world. Many money gurus have said that fortunes are built with other people's money. But if you are going to borrow to buy an asset, you have to remember that yes, it can magnify your gains but also your losses. Make sure you understand the worst-case scenarios. What if interest rates go up on your loan? What if you lost your job or something happened where you needed the money? What if your investment tanks? The reality is that you could lose money — and here you'd be losing money you don't have because you borrowed it.

"Okay, great, Melissa," you say. "I've got a strategy. Where do I find the money bombs to throw at this debt?"

Other than birthday money, tax refunds, work bonuses, inheritances or lottery wins, you'll probably have to cut expenses or earn it. Here's an excuse to go back and relive the joy of the previous chapters about budgeting and making more money.

YOUR HAPPY MONEY TO-DO LIST

- Freeze your credit card in a metaphorical block of ice (or a literal one, you do you!) and just use cash or your debit card. You can't be punching that debt in the morning, and slipping it treats in the evening — it's never going to die.
- Unsubscribe from your shopping emails and from Instagram accounts that promote shopping. Delete your group buying app and your food delivery app. Stay away from malls. Don't even tempt yourself with more debt when you're in combat mode.
- List your debts. Tackle the one with the highest interest rate.
- Call your credit card company and ask them for a lower interest rate. Tell them that you're thinking of switching to the Platinum Classic Plus card or whatever, because it is offering a rate of 8.99% and you're paying 19.99% on your outstanding balance. You don't ask, you don't get.
- If you're transferring your balance from one card to another with a lower interest rate, find out when the low-interest period ends. Create

a strict repayment schedule so you can get your balance the eff down within that window. Write down the deadline in your calendar and set an alarm as a reminder.

- Stress-test your budget. Look at how interest rate increases on your loans will affect your life and your ability to save for other goals. Look at what a 1% bump will do, what 2% will mean on your mortgage and your line of credit. If you can't stomach it, it might be time to get more aggressive on your outstanding debts.
- Order your credit file once a year from a credit bureau such as Equifax or TransUnion. It's free and will give you a rundown of your credit history. Make sure it's accurate. If you want your credit score for free, a number of sites offer it, including Credit Karma or RateHub.

MONEY TALKS

- Why do you have debt in the first place?
- What is worth going into debt for?
- If something is 90% off and costs $1,000 but you'd have to go into debt to take advantage of this sale, would you and why?
- What would you spend your money on if you didn't have debt payments?
- Would you consider buying a $400,000 home versus a $500,000 home (the cheaper one is smaller, outside of your target area or needs some fixing up) if it saved you $60,000 in interest over 25 years? If so, how would you rather spend that $60,000?

24
BULLETPROOF YOUR HAPPINESS

Thinking back, it would have been helpful if on the back of my marriage certificate, there was a disclaimer that said, "Shit's about to get real."

Mofo and I got married in October and by February, an entry in my journal reads, "I married Mofo. This person who is my husband is sort of like Mofo. He looks like Mofo. But he isn't."

During the worst times, I would lock myself in the bathroom to cry or go for a drive to scream because it all felt so unfair, and I felt so alone. I wanted to be reading books on pregnancy; I did not want to be talking to doctors about the side effects of psychotropic drugs. I wanted to be snuggling as newlyweds on the couch; I did not want to be holding my husband as he sobbed and begged for his suffering to end.

But during the worst times, I did not worry about money. I did not fear losing our new home. I did not stress about bills. Months before, we had paid off our wedding and skipped the honeymoon to save money. We chose to buy a townhouse that was well below our budget. We had disability insurance in case one of us could not work. Last, we had emergency funds set aside that we could use to pay for treatment if he needed it.

This was a gift. It gave me the space to breathe, to feel moments of peace and to regroup just enough to face another day with love, grace and self-respect. Because I didn't worry about money, I could focus on the thing that really mattered — helping my husband heal.

I've met many people who have hit financial hard times. And it was not because they had a latte addiction or because they didn't understand RRSP or IRA rules. Very early in my career, I wrote a newspaper series about homelessness and spent a month interviewing people in shelters, at food banks and on the streets. On another occasion, I spent every day for three months profiling a different family in need. And for years, I volunteered for a charity where I helped deliver gift boxes to underprivileged children at Christmas. Some of the individuals and families who I spoke with were living regular lives but got knocked into a cycle of poverty by a series of unfortunate events — an illness, an accident, a job loss. Maybe they were already barely treading water, swimming against systemic challenges such as stagnant wages or a lack of affordable housing, and then an unexpected wave swept them under.

Shit happens. We cannot control when and if shit will happen, but we can control how prepared we are for a shitstorm. And while thinking about bad shit happening feels pretty crappy, planning for a financial worst-case scenario can be an incredible stress reliever. Just think: when life suckerpunches you and you're still able to stand (and maybe flip it the bird), you'll be plenty happy.

Raccoons tore holes through your roof and it's going to cost $4,000 to fix it? No problem. You have an emergency fund. You hurt your back while showing your son that you can still do a cartwheel and now you can't work? You've got disability insurance to cover your bills. Finally, you've given up your dream of having a sparkly vampire gift you with eternal life and you're worried about your loved ones after you die? Your healthy self has qualified for life insurance, and your family's needs are covered.

Winter is coming

As a reporter, I inevitably wrote many, many stories about the weather. You'd think Canadians would be bored of news about snow. But nope. My thesaurus was dog-eared for easy access to the word "cold." And I know cold. I grew up in Winnipeg, one of the coldest cities on the planet, where before walking to school, I'd check the weather channel to see how long it would take for exposed skin to freeze. Frostbite in 10 minutes? Not bad. That gives me enough time to build a snowman first.

We devote a lot of time and resources preparing for cold weather — shovels, snowblowers, sidewalk salt, snow tires. We caulk our windows, we clean our gutters, we hide our patio cushions in storage boxes. My friends will put emergency kits in the car with blankets and handwarmers and survival kits at home with water and canned food in case a storm knocks out the power for a few days.

We get ready for snow every year, but many of us devote no energy to preparing for a financial winter. In the case of your life and your financial situation, we always think things are going to be sunny. But that's not how life works.

To prep for a financial winter, if you have high-interest consumer debt, make fighting it one of your top priorities. When you're down, debt will kick you. As I said, this might mean having a smaller emergency fund (of only one month's worth of living expenses) and allocating your extra cash to debt.

To start your emergency fund, create a monthly automatic money transfer into a separate account from your chequing account. If you can, give a nickname to that account/payee: "You got this" or "Bulletproofed." You'll want to aim for three months' worth of living expenses (which you'll have identified after listing your fixed expenses in your spending plan). If you're established in a stable career with little to no debt, or you have family or a partner who could help support you, you could aim for less. If you're a contract worker or freelancer, if you're not eligible for employment insurance, if you don't have any disability benefits through work or disability insurance, if you're the sole breadwinner in your family, you might want more. I know. That's a crap-ton of money. But try not to be discouraged. Just look at your own situation and what your needs would be and start this month.

You'll want to be able to access the money right away and at a low cost — in a high-interest savings account or redeemable guaranteed investment certificate (GIC) that allows you to cash out without a penalty, for example.

Some people choose to not have an emergency fund and keep a line of credit available in case of shit happening.

They argue that rather than having money sitting in a bank, getting very little interest, they'd rather have the money working for them — going to their mortgage or invested in a portfolio. If you have other savings available, investments that can be easily sold, you're debt-free and you have cash flow to handle interest payments, that might totally work for you.

But when shit happens, to me adding debt is like adding more shit.

Insurance, or incaseshit

"You got to have some insurance," comedian Chris Rock says. "They shouldn't even call it insurance, they should call it 'incaseshit.'"

Most of us get the need for car insurance. And most of us also get the importance of health insurance. But what about other kinds of insurance? I'm talking about life insurance and disability insurance. In an interview, I asked an insurance expert why he thought that younger adults don't think about life insurance or disability insurance. (Remember, I've always been a worrywart, so without insurance, I'd walk around with my butt painfully clenched, waiting for disaster.)

"Because they think they're Superman," he said.

I, of course, used the opportunity to dress up like Supergirl to do a financial video about the benefits of insurance. In it, I said that Superman could use disability insurance too. What if he got poked in the eye with a shard of kryptonite and couldn't work at *The Daily Planet* for a while? Insurance companies offer up all sorts of scary stats about your chances of becoming disabled; let's just say the odds are not in your favour and you could be disabled for months, even years. This is where disability insurance would help. If Superman could not work because of injury or illness, disability insurance would help cover his financial obligations; he still needs to eat and pay for his bachelor pad in Metropolis. He's a proud hero; he's not going to resort to robbery or launch a Kickstarter fund.

In fact, what if Superman applied for disability insurance? When providing Superman a quote, a bank or insurer would ask for his age (33), his height (6-foot-3), weight (235 pounds) and occupation (reporter/superhero). He'd tell them that while he's smoking hot, he doesn't smoke, and he'd admit to doing hazardous activities such as punching through buildings. Let's say Clark Kent makes about $4,535 a month. He could purchase a policy that would pay him $3,175 a month for up to five years (after a waiting period of 120 days).

To have this coverage in case shit happened, one bank quoted him a monthly premium of $84. Another otherwise healthy, non-smoking journalist who didn't fly into space to uppercut aliens might be $56 for the same coverage. Wonder Woman's premiums would be similar to $84. A 23-year-old lady who doesn't regularly fly an invisible plane would pay $58 for the same coverage.

If you rely on a paycheque, you should consider calling an insurance broker to shop around for the right policy or find out if your employer offers disability insurance in its benefits package and make sure you've signed up for it. You'll get it for a great discount through your employer; however, if you ever leave your job, you leave that benefit behind too.

When it comes to disability insurance, shop around. Compare quotes from various insurers. Work with an experienced insurance broker. Read reviews. Most disability insurance replaces up to 70% of your income for a specific period of time (sometimes a few years or to age 65 if you remain disabled).

There's a waiting period until that monthly payment begins — usually 60, 90 or 180 days (the longer the waiting period, the cheaper your insurance premiums). Here's where your emergency fund could help float you. Also, look at how the policy defines "disabled." Some will pay out if you can't perform the duties in your own occupation; some will pay out only if you can't work at all. (For example, your injuries may prevent you from professionally dancing, but because you could still be a telemarketer, there's no payout.)

Meanwhile, critical illness insurance is available if you become sick with a life-altering illness. If you survive a waiting period (great job), you'll receive a lump sum of cash to do with whatever you wish.

INSURANCE FOR EVERYTHING

Years ago, I was in Hawaii to perform at a salsa dancing festival, and I got food poisoning a few hours before the show. Moments before stepping on stage, I was in the bathroom and it was like a scene from The Exorcist, except the possessed girl was wearing a sequin bra and tassels. I danced. I bowed. And then I called my insurance company. Luckily, I had bought travel insurance before my trip. The company gave me a list of approved health care facilities to visit. My insurance covered my hospital stay and medicine, which ended up being thousands of dollars. Now my favourite photo from that trip is a picture of me in the hospital bed, giving a thumbs-up with an IV drip attached under my VIP festival wristband.

Needless to say, I'm a fan of insurance. (Maybe the least cool thing anyone could say, but one of the most money savvy.) Let's take a quick look at two other kinds of often overlooked insurance.

Pet insurance: My friend's cat once ate dental floss. The surgery to remove it cost $2,000, which she couldn't afford up front. Fortunately, the veterinary hospital had a payment plan, saving the cat's butt (and the rest of its GI tract). We love our fur babies, our scaly soulmates, our feathered friends, but we often underestimate how much medical procedures can cost if they become injured or eat stupid things. Pet insurance could help cover the costs. Monthly premiums can range from $35 to $80. The deductibles and limits will vary per plan. If you're shopping around, look for a policy that covers exams, consultation fees and taxes; you can even get coverage for dental care and preventative care. But look into the insurance company; read reviews. Owners have been caught off-guard before — having claims denied or having insurance premiums increase after making claims. In lieu of buying insurance, you could put aside money for your own pet insurance fund. You could take $50 every month per pet and put it in a designated savings account marked Fluffy or Fido.

Tenant's insurance: When I was a renter, I thought, "I don't own anything of value. And I'm a Scrabble-playing bookworm who works 18 hours a day, so it's unlikely I'll cause any property damage." I didn't get renter's insurance. But I should have. If I had lost all of my possessions in a fire, the cost to replace them would've been in the thousands. And if I had to move out while the landlord fixed the burned apartment, insurance would've covered my hotel stay. If I'd left the water running in a plugged bathtub and it overflowed, insurance could pay for damages. If someone was injured in my apartment — my dog mistook a person's arm for a T-bone and took a chomp, for example — insurance would cover the liability. Renter's insurance is cheap. Renter's remorse isn't.

Happily ever afterlife

Yes, all of your dreams are coming true. Another section about insurance!!! Look, I know there are innumerable things that we'd rather do than discuss insurance, laundry or dental work. Surveys show that even if we have life insurance, we think it's too complicated, too overwhelming, too boring, too depressing to talk about. We tend only to get it when we reach a milestone: starting your first job, buying your first home, getting married or having kiddies. I know people who think spending money on insurance is like cremating your money.

But here's a question: would your family be able to meet its everyday expenses if you or your spouse were to die? Yes, I intend to live forever too, but in the event that you die, who would your death affect financially? If no one is depending on you, then it's all good. But if you want to leave some money to take care of your loved ones, pay for your rocking farewell party and settle your debts (your mortgage, for example), then finding the right life insurance coverage would give you peace of mind.

If you think, "My fiancé can fend for himself. Maybe we'll get it when we have kids in 10 years," are you okay with the risk that you may not then be as mega fit as you are now? When you apply for a life insurance policy, most companies have an obligatory medical exam — someone shows up at your house to check you out, take your blood, etc.

I once interviewed a 32-year-old supply teacher who became diagnosed with ovarian cancer. She had no history of cancer in her family. She felt healthy. She is recovering but regrets that she's now unable to get the kind of life insurance coverage that she wants for her family. I know someone who applied for life insurance after his father passed away and discovered that his premiums were more expensive because of his family's health history.

The earlier you buy, the cheaper the premiums will be and the longer you'll be able to lock them in at that price for terms of 10, 15, 20, 25 or 30 years. For a healthy, non-smoking 25-year-old, $250,000 worth of life insurance coverage for a term of 25 years could cost about $25 a month. For a healthy, non-smoking 35-year-old, the same coverage would be about $35 a month, plus they spent a decade without the reassurance of coverage.

This is super gross — and I bear no ill will to this person decades later — but when I was in kindergarten, Jason Hale used to pick up dog poo on a stick and fling it at me. I was unprepared for shit then. Never again. I got disability insurance and life insurance in my mid-to late-20s; I was buying my condo, and I didn't want the bank's mortgage insurance (see the sidebar for why) so I got term life insurance to cover my mortgage in case I died. I qualified for the cheapest rate, which I've been paying ever since. I've actually added more insurance products as my needs have changed. So bring on the shitstorm. I'm armed with umbrellas.

Insurance-speak

I have a friend who is an insurance broker. And she's lovely. But when she starts talking about insurance, my eyes cross as I achieve boregasm. Insurance-speak is not for the faint of heart. But if I've learned anything from my reporter days, it's that you ask questions first and then determine what shots to take. Before you take a shot at a particular life insurance policy, ask your broker a few questions.

How much insurance coverage do I need to ensure that my favourite people are taken care of? At a minimum, it could be leaving no debts (covering your mortgage, your consumer debt) and providing some income to surviving loved ones. Or it could be providing money for infinite annual family trips to the Wizarding World of Harry Potter, where you've requested your ashes be scattered. Also, if you have a benefit plan at work that offers life insurance, take that amount into account, but be aware that if you leave that job, that coverage is gone.

What type do I need? Should I have term or permanent life insurance? With term insurance, you buy it for a period of time: 10, 20, 30, 100 years, etc. You assume that when the term ends, your family won't have a need for the money (you'll have savings, you'll have paid off/down the house, your kids are adults). Term insurance is affordable and, in most cases, sufficient to cover the needs of a family. With permanent insurance, it's, well, permanently in place until you die. When you die, your loved ones get paid. (The most common types are whole life insurance and universal life insurance.) It's good if you want to leave an inheritance for your family and/or you want to provide them with money to pay estate taxes. Permanent insurance allows you to invest money inside the policy; the investments grow in a tax-sheltered environment and can be given tax-free to your dependents when you die (in addition to the payout). Also, if you cancel your policy, you get some cash back.

Okay, if I'm buying term, what term is appropriate for me? Ten years, 20 years? If you choose a 10-year policy, which is inexpensive, it will come up for renewal when you are older and possibly less healthy. Twenty years is a better bet. If you get it when you're 30, in 20 years, hopefully your debts will be paid off, your kid will be headed to university and you'll have some savings.

If I'm buying term insurance, is it convertible to permanent insurance? Convertible term life insurance means that (up to a certain age) you can switch your term policy to a permanent policy without a medical exam. This is important because what if you become ill during your 20-year term, for example, and new coverage would be way more expensive or, worse, unavailable to you?

FOUR REASONS WHY LIFE INSURANCE WINS OVER MORTGAGE INSURANCE

When you buy a home and you're happily signing all of your mortgage documents, your bank or mortgage lender will probably ask you if you want mortgage life insurance or mortgage protection life insurance. (This is different from private mortgage insurance or mortgage default insurance, which is required when you put less than 20% down as a down payment.) Mortgage life insurance pays the balance of your mortgage to the bank if you die.

It sounds like a great idea, like when the salesman explains the benefits of the extended warranty for your new gadget. But here's why applying for term life insurance to cover your mortgage is a better option.

- Mortgage insurance is generally more expensive than term life insurance.
- Mortgage insurance may offer you coverage without a medical exam. (They'll ask you a few questions and decide whether you qualify for insurance.) But when you (or your loved ones) make a claim, this is when they'll contact your doctors and check into your medical history. Buyer beware. They can decide that, despite the fact that you've paid premiums, you never

qualified for a payout and they will not cover the mortgage.

- As you pay down your mortgage, you'll continue to pay the same premiums for mortgage insurance, even though the payout grows smaller and smaller.
- Mortgage insurance pays the bank. With term life insurance, the money goes to your loved one. They will have the flexibility to choose how to spend that money, including paying off the mortgage if they want.

My cat inherits it all

You might be thinking, "Create a will? Bleh. That's the last thing I need."

Actually, yes, that *is* one of the last things you'll need in life. If you die without a will, the law says you have died "intestate." It sounds like you've suffered a fatal bowel movement, but it means you've left no instructions for how to divide and distribute your stuff. In these circumstances, the law decides who gets what. (That just triggers my inner control freak.) A will ensures that your wishes are carried out and gives you peace of mind.

You can get do-it-yourself kits and books, but you have to make sure you have the right documents for your jurisdiction. If you've downloaded the will from the internet, for example, is it for your province or state?

And if you've made your own will, it could be fraught with problems. Have you signed and had it witnessed on the same day? Does it have contingencies? For example, if you leave all your money to your sister, what if your sister dies before you? To avoid reality-TV level drama in your family, a good estate lawyer will walk you through the process. Some offer a free consultation; the will could cost you a few hundred dollars to $1,000, depending on the complexity of your situation. A lawyer will also be able to help you with special clauses and circumstances.

In Ontario, for example, you can put a clause in your will that protects the money that is made from an inheritance in case your child and their spouse divorce. Or if you have a child collecting government benefits, you need a special provision in your will for your child, otherwise, they could be cut off from those government benefits.

If you have a simple estate and you want to go the DIY route, some low-cost solutions that help you create legal wills without visiting lawyers are LegalWills.ca (custom documents start at about $40) or Willful.co, (it costs between $99 to $250) or for Americans, Quicken WillMaker, a do-it-yourself software program ($69.99).

A few things to think about when creating a will. List your assets. Decide who gets what and when. Consider who you want to be guardian for your child, then choose an alternate, just in case. Do you want your child to get all the money at 18? Or in instalments, say some at 18, then 25 and 30? Choose an executor; this person is responsible for managing your affairs after you die (taking care of your assets until your son becomes an adult, for example) and carrying out the wishes in your will (having your brain cryogenically frozen so superior future beings can cure what ails you).

You'll also want to create a living will, which sounds like an oxymoron. But it's for when you're alive but you're not able to make decisions for yourself or your property. By creating a living will or a power of attorney document, you're appointing someone else to act on your behalf. Who do you want that person to be?

And to the cat lovers out there, unfortunately you can't leave your estate to your feline, but you can make sure that a caretaker has money to look after your kitty if your life runs out before her nine lives.

The other difficult "talk" to have with your parents

As a joke (that I recorded for educational purposes and online dissemination), I called my parents and asked them about estate planning.

"Hi Mom . . . do you have a will and am I getting all of your stuff?"

"Hi Dad. Do you like vegetables? Yes? Okay, have you ever given any thought to what would happen if you became one?"

Obviously, this is not the way to talk to your parents about their affairs. However, it is still a crucial talk. Yes, it may hurt to think about the day when they will not be around. And yes, it might seem like you're counting their money. But perhaps start with talking about your concerns and your fears and asking if they've made any arrangements. "With most difficult conversations, we have to make sure it comes from a place of love. 'Because I love you, because I always want to do what's in your best interest, I want to have this conversation,'" suggests Kathy Kortes-Miller, author of *Talking About Death Won't Kill You.*

My most meaningful conversation on this matter started when I created my first will and I asked my father for advice. I asked if he had a power of attorney and what his wishes would be. (His original answer about liking vegetables is bull. I've never seen him eat anything that wasn't a shade of beige or brown.)

Kortes-Miller says to look for times to bring up the talk or find "teachable moments." When Kortes-Miller's aunt died unexpectedly, her father, as the executor, faced a lot of work, including getting a dumpster to clean out her home. "Every once in a while, I'll say to him, 'You're not going to do that to me, right?'" Kortes-Miller says. "He'll laugh. That's when he shows me his files and reminds me where his passwords are."

Ask where your parents keep their important documents. If you need help getting organized, consider a legacy planning product like Future File ($100); it comes with a manual, a guidebook and a file folder to help organize your parents' wishes and information.

It's an unpleasant talk, no doubt. But on the other side of that unpleasantness is peace of mind.

YOUR HAPPY MONEY TO-DO LIST

- Build your bulletproof suit. Create a monthly automatic money transfer into a separate account called "Incaseshit." If you have high-interest consumer debt, tackle that first.
- Talk to an insurance broker about your disability, critical illness and life insurance needs.
- Get some insurance quotes. Sites like InsurEye.com provide quotes for insurance products as well as consumer reviews.
- Ask your family and friends for a referral to an estate lawyer or email a few reputable ones in your area. Check out an online will company.

- If you created your will years ago, make sure it's up-to-date. Is the executor that you named still alive/still your friend? Did you make a will before your other kid was born and she's not named?
- Talk to your loved ones about their end-of-life plans and wishes.

MONEY TALKS

- If you lost your job tomorrow, how long would you be able to cover your bills and support yourself or your family?
- If you slipped and fell during some overzealous half-time dancing at a sports event in the U.K. and the hospital bill was $6,000, how would you pay it?
- If you were not around, who would be affected financially by your absence and how?

THE LIFE-CHANGING MAGIC
OF GIVING A BUCK

Share your joy and you'll always be rich.

25
GIVE TO GET

My grandfather lived with us until he died at the age of 92. His bedroom was filled with plaques and photos of him shaking hands with mayors and other dignitaries. When I was little, I thought, "People really like the chow mein at Gung Gung's restaurant." As I grew older, I understood that he was being honoured for a lifetime of philanthropy.

I've always tried to be giving. When I didn't have money, I regularly gave my blood (I've got the good stuff — O negative, the universal donor blood type). I gave my time, volunteering whenever I could, rolling pennies, mentoring new immigrants, organizing clothing drives for families. But I've sometimes felt aimless with my giving, especially when it came to donating money.

A way to buy happiness is to spend it on other people, but we can make a bigger impact on our happiness and on the world with our dollars.

We just need to begin with one question: what causes do you care about most? Then let's talk about how much, when, who to give to and how to know where your money is going.

Give and get pleasure

Mofo gives money away. Often, he'll come home with a story of how he helped someone that day. A young man asked him for change so he took him into a restaurant for a meal. A woman struggling with her baby in the grocery line had forgotten her wallet so he paid for her groceries. Shortly after meeting my cousins, he disappeared into a Chinese bakery with an elderly panhandler; we stood around awkwardly on the street while she decided on an array of buns and pastries.

"Is this guy for real?" their faces asked. Yeah. And he would've done it even if no one was looking.

Our immediate family members have poked fun at him. "Are you rich or something that you have so much money to give away?" "Are you sure they even deserved it?"

They're missing the point. Mofo is also getting something from these acts. Don't they see how happy it makes him?

There is a clear link between giving to others and happiness. Whether you're rich or poor, worldwide surveys show that donating to charity makes you feel more satisfied with life and makes you feel wealthier.

Our brains are hardwired to act selflessly and to be generous. An economist at University of Oregon placed test subjects in an fMRI scanner and they were shown a computer monitor with the option to donate anywhere from $15 to $45 from a $100 cash fund to a food bank. Even when money was involuntarily taken from the fund to be donated, a part of the brain associated with processing rewards lit up. When the subjects donated voluntarily, their pleasure zones lit up even more.

In their own experiment, professors Elizabeth Dunn and Michael Norton gave people $5 and $20 to spend by 5 p.m. that day. Some were told to spend the money on a gift for themselves or to pay a bill while others were asked to buy a gift for someone else or give to charity. Those who spent the money on others were happier when interviewed later. Dunn also talked to workers at a Boston firm before and after they received a bonus that averaged about $5,000. The most important predictor of their happiness was how they spent the money — and if they spent it on others.

Giving makes you feel connected to others, even strangers. When you feel like your money has had a clear impact on the world, on someone else's life and on their happiness, there's no way to put a price on that.

When you buy clothing for yourself, you're trying to change your self-perception from the outside. But when you spend money on others, you're changing your self-perception from the inside.

My love language, according to Gary Chapman's popular book *The 5 Love Languages*, has always been gift giving. My parents don't praise. We don't hug. But my mom would sew me beautiful clothing and my dad gave me treats. I will spend hours wrapping gifts for others. People with good social relationships are happier, healthier and live longer. Giving to loved ones can strengthen relationships. No one is suggesting that you try to buy someone's love with gifts, but money spent on others is always money well spent if it boosts your own well-being.

The Melissa Leong Shoe Foundation

When I was younger, I just waited until others approached me for donations, but now I've found it's more empowering to make my own choices. So when the cashier asks at the checkout if I'd like to donate $1 to their cause, I can say, "No, thank you," without feeling like a monster, because I'm choosing to support something else.

Choose the causes that reflect your personal beliefs and values. What is lighting a fire in you at the moment? Do you ache at the sight of starving polar bears roaming the Arctic? Are you inspired by your mother's fight against cancer?

Next, search for charities that meet your criteria. You need to make sure the charity is registered, then you'll want to do further research to see that your donation won't be wasted. The truth is it costs money to run these charities. For example, if you donate $100 to the Melissa Leong Shoe Foundation, $40 might go to cover fundraising costs, another $10 might go to administration costs. That means only half of your donation goes to the needy cause.

Before you give, check with online charity evaluators or publications that rate organizations and give you a breakdown of how they spend your money. (Check out CharityWatch.org for the U.S. and CharityIntelligence.ca for Canada.) You'll want to see that your charity is spending at least 65% or more of its budget on charitable programs and services.

Finally, watch out for fraudsters who will take advantage of your kindness. If you get a phone call from a charity and you like what you hear, hang up, do some research and contact the charity directly. If you get an unsolicited email, don't click any links. If you're donating online, make sure that the site you're using is secure before sharing any personal information.

Account for generosity

Once you figure out which worthy causes you're most passionate about and which charities you'd like to support, you should set an annual budget. Make it a priority and automatically set aside a certain amount every month.

How much you give is completely up to you. Some religious groups suggest that you give 10% of your income to charity. In reality, however, Canadians give just under 1% of our annual income to good causes.

After looking at your charity budget, whatever it may be, I'd break it up. Maybe you decide that 50% of your available funds is going to your charity or charities of choice, 30% is going to your community or religious organization and the remaining 20% is available for unplanned gifts, such as disaster relief or a friend's online fundraising drive.

Keep in mind that spreading your money among multiple organizations could diminish the bang for your buck. More of your money could be going to pay for processing expenses and administrative and fundraising fees. On the other hand, from a happiness perspective, we get more pleasure from giving $100 to 10 different charities than from donating $1,000 to one. A compromise would be to donate $100 every month to your charity of choice. Automatic monthly donations will be easier for you to manage, and charities can make longer-term plans with your money.

Most of us give lump sums to charities in December while we're in the spirit of giving and we're taking stock of our finances for the year. But resources tend to be scarcer during the holidays, and we tend to give less in a one-time lump sum than we would if we were to spread out our donations over the year. Consider automating your giving, as you do with your saving, so that everyone wins.

Make the most of your donations

Don't forget to get a receipt. This is how you'll document your donation for tax purposes.

In the United States, you can generally deduct contributions up to 50% (20% or 30% in some cases) of your adjusted gross income. If you made $50,000 one year and donated $5,000 to charities, your income for tax purposes would be $45,000.

In Canada, you get a 15% federal tax credit on the first $200 that you donate. On total amounts over $200, you get a 29% tax credit. On top of this, you'll get provincial tax credits, which vary from province to province. A credit reduces the amount of taxes you pay; if you don't owe taxes in one year, wait until you do to claim your donations. A good strategy to go over that $200 mark is to combine two or more years' worth of donations (up to a maximum of five years). You might also consider combining your donation receipts with your spouse and having one person claim them on one return.

In times of crisis, you may want to donate food products, clothing and other used items. But unless an organization is doing a particular drive, that kind of philanthropy is not always efficient because there may not be infrastructure set up to organize and distribute items to the needy. It might be more helpful to have a garage sale of your used items and then donate that money to a good cause. For example, a food bank can purchase groceries for rock-bottom bulk prices, so giving cash over canned tuna is way better.

Also, look into giving through your workplace because some have giving campaigns where the money comes from automatic payroll deductions; some employers even match your contributions.

And if you wish you had more money to give, how about taking other people's money? Create a Facebook fundraiser or host your own fundraising event. In lieu of birthday presents, ask for donations. Make something, sell it and donate the proceeds. Run a marathon or do your own challenge. My editor's friend watches one horror movie a day for a month and blogs about it; people who donate money get to pick the movie. How about that? Scares that care.

You definitely should brag about this

A good friend sponsors a toddler in a low-income country and her social media posts about it are the highlight of my day. Another friend recently wrote on her Facebook wall, "Confused about which local charity to give my money to. Does anyone have suggestions?" Now there's a humblebrag we should all get behind. What followed was a torrent of great suggestions, including many local projects that I had never heard of.

This is the opposite of putting your hand out and asking for money; this is you bragging about how generous you are and it's awesome. It will hopefully inspire others to do the same.

YOUR HAPPY MONEY TO-DO LIST

- Choose a cause or many causes that resonate with you.

- Look up some charities that support that cause. Use online charity evaluators or publications that investigate and rate charities. Make sure they're registered and make sure you collect and file away your receipt for tax purposes.
- Determine how much you want to give to your charities.
- Tell everyone about your generosity. Tweet. Post. Snap. Put something good into this world.

MONEY TALKS

- If you could make the world better today, what three things would you tackle first?
- What is one of the most generous gifts you've given? What is one of the most generous deeds you've done? How did those make you feel?

HAPPY ENDING

In the months leading up to this book's deadline, Mofo and I were happy. Business was good. We finally had a routine of work, school, gym/hockey that felt fulfilling. But the best part? We were expecting our second kid. Our son wore his "big brother" T-shirt to surprise his grandparents, and he was already talking about how his sibling could share his room (but not his toys).

But on Christmas Day, as the family gathered for turkey and Secret Santa, I started to bleed. I had had two previous miscarriages before our son was born, but this one still shocked and wounded me.

January gave us no time to process. Germs invaded our home. We had pink eye. Strep throat. Influenza. I left the house five times in 30 days, once to go to my best friend's birthday while wearing a surgical mask and the other times to see doctors. I wore a parka inside to stop fever chills while playing trains with my equally feverish kid. All day, we made what my mom calls snot dumplings, filling tissue with slime (the only time dumplings don't make me happy).

Meanwhile, Mofo (with pink eye and a terrible cold) was out of the house, tending to his father who had dislocated his shoulder falling down a flight of stairs and then, two weeks later, cut himself falling through a sheet of glass. A week after that, a close family member received devastating health news.

We felt pulverized. And our impulse was to heal it with money. Mofo started talking about spending thousands of dollars on another pinball machine for his man cave. Meanwhile, I felt like Gollum, or some swamp-dwelling troll. I was snotty and sweaty and my face was cracked and crusted like tree bark. I started talking about how I'd get a haircut, colour and a facial. (I don't even like facials — the closest thing in my life to a facial is when I open a steamy dishwasher immediately after a cycle.) I also looked into buying new cosmetics and a $200 anti-aging cream that my friend recommended. I wanted to be a beautiful, healthy version of me again. Someone who wasn't sick, someone who, just maybe, could have a healthy pregnancy.

We had to give our brains a shake. No! *No*. We know better. We know that we can't flip the happy switch with our credit cards. We know that rather than wipe the pain away, these purchases will just sit on the surface before sinking into our murk.

Instead, I meditated and worked out. I stuck affirmations on my mirror. I asked my best friend to babysit so that Mofo and I could go on a date and laugh and connect. I booked a session with a therapist. I looked into a family vacation. And I organized a day-trip with my girls.

The thing is there is no such thing as happily ever after. Just after. And more after if you're lucky. It's up to us to face every day with a commitment to do our best and to make the most of it. Every moment is a chance to recalibrate. Sometimes, especially in the curves and dips of life, we forget what will truly make us happy. That's okay. It's in the mistakes and in the challenges that we can discover and rediscover our happy powers.

I'm so happy and proud that you've taken this journey with me and that you've reached the end of this book. (If you've just skipped to the end, oh man, you missed when I revealed the secret to success in the fourth chapter, or maybe it was the seventh . . .) It's no easy feat to finish a finance book. High-five, Happy Money Ninja.

The world will keep telling us that happiness is spelled with dollar signs. My hope is that I've added another voice to your head or strengthened the one that's always been there. It says, "I know better. I know what fulfills me. I know what is valuable in my life. I am in control. Let's do this."

THE LAST THINGS ON YOUR HAPPY MONEY TO-DO LIST

- Write yourself a letter to be opened in three months. In it, include at least three major points that you've taken away from this book. Write to future you what you hope you'll always remember. Write a few things that you hope you will have accomplished in three months. Seal it and put it away, then set a calendar reminder to open the letter in three months. Or put your address and a stamp on it and give it to a friend or someone in your OHM tribe to mail to you in three months.

- Tell someone about your recent money accomplishments (and the whole story including the struggles, the epiphanies, the wins), even if it's simply that you read this great book.
- If you enjoyed this book, please consider doing me an act of kindness and review, recommend or post about it. If you didn't enjoy it, please refer back to the chapter about having no regrets and moving on with your life.

MONEY TALKS

- Enough talking. It's go time.

CONNECT WITH ME

Email me to tell me how the journey is going, to hire me to speak at your event, for bulk book orders or for partnerships. (If you're a Nigerian prince, absolutely I can help you deposit that money.)

- hello@melissaleong.com

Follow me on Instagram for more money tips and photos of food I've burned:

- instagram.com/lisleong

Follow me on Twitter for more money tips and funny GIFs from '90s sitcoms:

- twitter.com/lisleong

Follow me on Facebook for . . . to be honest, I'm not on Facebook very often. But when I am, I share amazing stuff.

- facebook.com/melissa.w.leong

Visit MelissaLeong.com for resources and other things you and your OHM tribe may need to continue kicking ass at life.

RESOURCES

If you're all in and want to go for your happy money black belt, here are some books, apps and podcasts worth checking out to help you level up and lighten up.

Books

To further boost your money savvy:

- *The Wealthy Barber Returns: Significantly Older and Marginally Wiser, Dave Chilton Offers His Unique Perspectives on the World of Money* by David Chilton
- *Stop Over-Thinking Your Money!: The Five Simple Rules of Financial Success* by Preet Banerjee
- *Worry-Free Money: The Guilt-Free Approach to Managing Your Money and Your Life* by Shannon Lee Simmons
- *Money Rules: Rule Your Money or Your Money Will Rule You* by Gail Vaz-Oxlade

To raise your happiness quotient:

- *10% Happier: How I Tamed the Voice in My Head, Reduced Stress Without Losing My Edge, and Found Self-Help That Actually Works — A True Story* by Dan Harris
- *Hardwiring Happiness: The New Brain Science of Contentment, Calm, and Confidence* by Dr. Rick Hanson
- *Happy Money: The New Science of Smarter Spending* by Elizabeth Cullen Dunn and Michael Norton
- *The Five-Minute Journal* by Intelligent Change

Podcasts

To stay up to date on the newest trends in fintech to the best strategies for paying down debt:

- *Moolala: Money Made Simple with Bruce Sellery* on Sirius XM
- *So Money* with Farnoosh Torabi
- *Mo' Money* with Jessica Moorhouse

To get more life-changing happiness tips and listen your way to better habits:

- *Happier* with Gretchen Rubin

Apps and online tools

To beef up your financial literacy:

- Kiplinger.com
- GetSmarterAboutMoney.ca

To budget like a champ:

- Mint
- Wally.me
- You Need a Budget (YNAB)

For a money app that's also a happiness coach:
- FindJoy.com

To keep your sanity and your receipts:
- Receipts by Wave

To run your own accounting department:
- Freshbooks

To set up your estate plan:
- Willful.co
- LegalWills.ca
- Quicken WillMaker
- FutureFile.com

To test yourself happy and for the latest in positive psychology:
- AuthenticHappiness.org

To track your screen time:
- Moment (inthemoment.ios)

To get grateful:
- Bliss (for Android)

To meditate:
- Stop Breathe & Think: Meditate
- Headspace

ACKNOWLEDGEMENTS

As a believer in the joy-boosting power of gratitude, I feel like thanking every person who had anything to do with this book, even tangentially. From you, the reader — even if you've picked this up on a coffee table to just read the acknowledgements (that's weird, but you do you) — to the guy walking by the coffee shop scratching his butt who inspired my crotch-itch joke.

But some deserve extra gratitude.

I want to thank my agent, Haskell Nussbaum, for hanging around for years while I promised to write this book.

Every writer needs an editor who, like Rumpelstiltskin, will weave straw into gold. I can't imagine having a better editor, collaborator, all-round-amazing human in my corner than Jen Knoch. If you'd be my editor, I'd write a million books.

Thank you to the incredible team at ECW Press for being champions of my book. It's really about the journey and you've made it awesome. Jessica Albert, your talent and keen eye (and your freakish focus with candy and tweezers) astound me; thank you for creating this cover.

To my friends at *The Social*, when I see the hashtag #womenempoweringwomen, I immediately think of all of you and your tremendous support.

There's no greater group of people than those at the *National Post*. (Posties forever.) AMO, you gave me a place, even after I chose to leave. Thank you to my former editors, Steve Meurice and Grant Ellis, who gave me the gift of the personal finance beat. You're like my career fairy godfathers. To my former finance editor, Suzanne Steel, thank you for nurturing my creativity and expanding my mind — I never imagined that writing about money would be so damn fun. To the A&L posse, the super team, you continue to inspire and cheerlead.

The personal finance crew in Canada is amazing. Thank you for every bit of advice about this journey and for your friendship. Money guru Bruce Sellery came up with the fantastic title of this book. For the rest of our lives, coffee is on me.

Thank you, Lorne Zeiler, for checking my numbers and for warning me about what bores your fledgling finance students.

A long, long list of friends and loved ones took the time to review bits of this book, and I'll thank you in person to avoid looking like I just won best actress and I'm breathlessly running through names while they play the music over my voice. I'm here for you anytime, for anything. Except if it's illegal and happens earlier than 7 a.m.

I am so grateful for a girl squad who stands by me and holds me up. You're like a personal team of superheroes, always saving my world — and sometimes rescuing me from myself.

Thank you, Duong Ramon, the Gayle to my Oprah. Thanks for listening to my stories for 25 years and for putting everything aside to read and line edit my entire manuscript. You were the smartest and kindest person I knew at 13. Still are.

To my family, my extended family and my in-laws, thank you for your love and enduring support.

And last but definitely not least, Sean. You're a strong, supportive mofo.

INDEX

ABOUT THE AUTHOR

Melissa Leong is a personal finance writer, keynote speaker, on-air personality and bestselling author. She briefly considered calling this book *Well*, so then everyone would say, "*Well* written by Melissa Leong."

She's the resident money expert on Canada's leading daytime talk show *The Social* and served as the personal finance reporter for the *Financial Post*. She regularly shares her savings tips on radio and television programs, and through her channels, she reaches millions in a quest to help them manage their money while maximizing happiness.

Over the last 15 years, she has covered a variety of subjects including crime, politics, terrorism, arts and business for the *National Post*, the *Toronto Star* and the *Globe and Mail*. She has profiled survivors of the Rwandan genocide, investigated nanny abuse in Hong Kong and interviewed thousands of subjects, including heads of state, royalty and celebrities such as Hugh Jackman and Carrie Fisher.

In her spare time, she mentors youth and volunteers for organizations that promote the advancement and empowerment of young women. She's also fully prepared for a zombie invasion and, if that doesn't occur, she's happily saving for retirement and for her kid's education.